Onwards and Upwards

How can teachers ensure that the transition from the Early Years Foundation Stage (EYFS) to Key Stage One is a positive experience for children? What are the issues for children, parents and teachers and how should teachers respond to these?

This book introduces the concept of transition and identifies the key problem areas for children and adults, focusing on the differences in philosophy and practice between the EYFS and Key Stage One, whilst also giving emphasis to the opportunities that are provided by the transition process. It stresses the need for a balanced approach and the importance of sustained shared thinking from the EYFS through Key Stage One and provides practical strategies for achieving this.

Onwards and Upwards includes detailed guidance on:

- preparing for the transition to Key Stage One
- the role of the teacher
- the balance between adult-led and child-initiated activity
- play and the use of the outdoor environment
- creating a stimulating environment that supports a balanced approach.

Throughout the book Kathleen Orlandi emphasises the child's perspective and draws on naturalistic observations of children before, during and after a period of transition. With case studies, key quotes from children, examples of practice and suggestions for planning, and questions for reflective practice, this textbook will be invaluable for students and practitioners in the EYFS and Key Stage One, as well as those responsible for continual professional development (CPD).

Kathleen Orlandi is Senior Lecturer in Childhood Studies at Liverpool Hope University. She is also Lead Manager of the North West Early Years Transformation Group (NWEYTG), which provides courses for candidates wishing to achieve Early Years Professional Status.

Onwards and Upwards

Supporting the transition to Key Stage One

Kathleen Orlandi

Routledge
Taylor & Francis Group

LONDON AND NEW YORK

First published 2012
by Routledge
2 Park Square, Milton Park, Abingdon, Oxon OX14 4RN

Simultaneously published in the USA and Canada
by Routledge
711 Third Avenue, New York, NY 10017

Routledge is an imprint of the Taylor & Francis Group, an informa business

British Library Cataloguing in Publication Data
A catalogue record for this book is available from the British Library

Library of Congress Cataloging in Publication Data
Orlandi, Kathleen.
Supporting the transition to Key Stage 1 / Kathleen Orlandi.
   p. cm.
   1. Early childhood education—Great Britain. 2. Promotion (School)—Great Britain. I. Title.
   LB1139.3.G7O75 2011
   372.210973—dc22   2011015170

ISBN: 978-0-415-61242-5 (hbk)
ISBN: 978-0-415-61243-2 (pbk)
ISBN: 978-0-203-80195-6 (ebk)

Typeset in Bembo
by HWA Text and Data Management, London

Printed and bound in Great Britain by
TJ International Ltd, Padstow, Cornwall

Contents

Illustrations

Figures

Tables

Acknowledgements

My grateful thanks to all the children and adults I have met and worked with for many years; they have provided challenges and so much learning! I hope that their messages of life's experiences in schools can be shared through this book, to help those in charge to reflect on their provision. Through this book it is my wish that the wisdom and experience of the children and adults I have encountered will be passed on to those who are also on a journey of reflection and development.

Introduction

Chapter content

This chapter defines the overall aims of the book and briefly introduces the nature of the research that informs it.

It takes a broad look at the aspects of transition for children moving from the Foundation Stage to Key Stage One. These include transition as an everyday experience for children, multi-dimensional influences on transition, what research says about transition to Key Stage One, and transition and the curriculum. These will be examined in greater depth in the following chapters.

The overall aims of the book

This book takes account of some of the issues and perceived barriers to successful transition from Foundation Stage to Year One in England, for children and adults. However, greater attention is given to the opportunities presented by this period of transition between two phases of education. This includes opportunities for critical reflection, challenging current practice, deeper pedagogical understanding and improved practice.

This book aims to bridge the gap between academic study, research and practice. It is hoped that it will inspire practitioners to engage in action research and collaborative research.

The nature of the research that informs much of the book

In addition to published research about transition or aspects of practice affected by transition, the examples used within the chapters are from the author's research. The examples are taken from small case studies in which several children were studied before, during and after transition from Reception Class to Year One. The reader should be aware that the children in the case study examples are all boys. However, there is no intention to address gender difference within this book. The case studies are real examples but the names of settings and children have been changed.

What about transition?

Transition as an everyday experience for children

Children go through various phases of transition in the first years of their lives. Many young children make transitions between carers and environments several times each day or across a week. For example, a child may be woken from his sleep by a parent and collected by a grandparent who then takes him to nursery or school. In school he will probably have a set of adults including a teacher who will care for him, except at lunchtime when a different team takes over. At the end of the day, the child will be collected by a relative or childminder and taken home, as the parents may be at work. This scenario may not be a real example, but is very typical of the experience of many children who have been in my care. For some children the changes across the day are even more confusing because of the use of breakfast and afternoon clubs. Some young children may attend two different Foundation Stage settings, for instance attending a playgroup in the morning and a maintained nursery in the afternoon. Transition from Foundation Stage to Key Stage One is just one more experience of change for children. With the introduction of the Foundation Stage there has been concern about the perceived gap between its curriculum and that of Key Stage One, and the consequent difficulties in transition between the two. This book focuses on this particular period of transition.

Multi-dimensional influences on transition

Dockett *et al.* (1999) studied the views of parents and educators about what is important about children's transition to school. They found that the majority of parents and educators wanted children to be happy, feel positive, and settle into school routines easily. However, they discovered that the experiences that were part of the transition were 'multi-dimensional', and that different children experience the same process in different ways as they make adjustments to different people, routines and contexts. They suggest that the geographic context is a crucial factor that affects the transition experience, but that the ways people respond to the issues of transition varied within geographical locations. Factors affecting this might include the length of time and mode of travel to the setting, or the distance between the locations of the pre-school and Key Stage One building, or even the nature of the layout and organisation. Other factors might include the variety of pre-school settings the children have attended before entering the school setting so that the children and families are not familiar with each other. They concluded that successful transition programmes would look quite different, as they would be responding to the local community needs.

The path children take across the Foundation Stage, and beyond it, varies. They often have a combination of playgroups and nurseries. However, individual arrangements were made for the remaining children whose needs varied. Some local authorities have guidelines in place, but flexibility must be a necessity. This may include a meeting for parents with the 'new' teachers, and visits of the children to their new classrooms to meet their 'new' teachers.

What research says about transition to Key Stage One

The transition from Foundation Stage to Key Stage One has been the subject of research commissioned by the Department for Education and Skills (DfES). One such research report (IFF, 2004) found that specific issues identified by settings were training and sharing of information. There was some dissatisfaction with the training offered by local authorities. Just over half of those interviewed said that they felt the transition had been very effective. Two areas of concern were: involvement of parents was identified as least effective in the process; and the Early Years practitioners were unsure of the outcomes of the transition process, and therefore felt unable to say if it had been effective.

Research commissioned by the DfES on transition was by the National Foundation for Educational Research (NFER), in which the views of children, parents and practitioners were sought (Sanders *et al.*, 2005). This research found that the biggest challenge identified by teachers was the move from a play–based curriculum to a more structured approach. The introduction to the literacy and numeracy lessons was cited as an example of a problem in that it was difficult to get children to sit and listen to the adult. The ability to sit still and listen to the teacher was identified by school staff as a key skill needed by children if they were to make a good start in Year One. Generally it was felt that the children coped well with the transition. For many children this is a positive thing as it is a demarcation of phases, and they celebrate moving 'up' to the next phase, and being at 'big school'. The research found that the younger/less mature children and those with special needs encountered most difficulties. Children's views revealed that they were unhappy with the loss of opportunities to learn through play, and they valued their experiences in Reception Class. They were worried about the amount of writing expected in Year One, and about having to sit still. The main negative aspect from parents was the lack of information about transition; they would have liked to have met the Year One teacher before the event, and would have liked to have received information about change in practice so they could prepare their child (Sanders *et al.*, 2005.) This lack of involvement with parents had also been identified as a key issue by IFF Research (IFF, 2004). The NFER research also found that there was a strongly expressed desire for training for Key Stage One teachers in how to provide for the transition from the Foundation Stage. The Foundation Stage curriculum guidance (DfEE, 2000) endorsed the practice of learning through play. Perhaps the Key Stage One teachers need reassurance that they too can use play and experiential learning for their classes.

The National Numeracy and Literacy Strategies were found to have been effective in providing guidance for the transition, but in some Year One Classes there was overemphasis on these at the expense of other aspects of the curriculum. The Reception Class teachers were under pressure from their colleagues in Key Stage One, and school management teams, to work towards the end of Key Stage One assessments, in which: 'The curriculum shift may be shown to have gone too far in terms of the prescription of a single pedagogical formula, in particular for Literacy and Numeracy' (David, 2003: 9).

Transition and the curriculum

Personal observation and communication with teachers currently working in the Foundation Stage indicates that this pressure has eased in many settings because:

> Early Years practitioners have been given permission, if they needed it, to plan a curriculum on what is known about developing children's understanding and learning. As a bonus, the whole of the Reception Year is included in the Foundation Stage and these children also now have a curriculum more suited to meeting their needs.
>
> (English, 2001: 197)

There have been issues with the Foundation Stage Profile (DfES, 2003). Although the handbook acknowledges that many judgements about children's progress can be made through the practitioner's knowledge of that child, and that occasionally there may be a need for additional planned observations, the latter seems to have been preferred by some practitioners. Personal experience working with colleagues confirms this, as does Ofsted's report on transition between Foundation Stage and Key Stage One (Ofsted, 2004). Ofsted found that few Year One teachers were using the profiles for planning, suggesting that this may be because of the 'absence of clear transitional links between the Foundation Stage curriculum and the subjects of the National Curriculum' (Ofsted, 2004). I suggest that the large number of records kept by some Foundation Stage teachers, as observed by Ofsted (2004) were perhaps off-putting. 'Schools were not doing enough to make sure that their assessments and recordings were of direct value' (Ofsted, 2004), and were advised to review the number and type of assessment used, taking into consideration requirements for Year One. Ofsted (2004) also recommend that subject coordinators are involved in planning for continuity between the two key stages. This may help to remove the imbalance mentioned above.

Discuss
- What types of transition do young children go through each day and each week?
- How many adults take care of them at different times of the day?
- Is there continuity in the way the children are cared for?
- Do the children exhibit anxiety when in transition from one carer to another?

Key messages
- Issues vary between locations and settings;
- Early Years teachers do not know about the outcomes of transition to the next phase;
- Parents want to be informed;
- The biggest issue is movement from a play-based approach to a more structured approach;
- Children generally view the transition as a positive experience to look forward to;
- Key Stage One teachers need to know more about the Foundation Stage approach.

The following chapters look at the issues relating to transition for the children and then for adults. Chapter 4 attempts to question whether it is the nature of preparation for transition or the change in practice that creates these issues for children and adults. Chapter 5 looks at the features of successful transition and provides two case studies in the same school to examine why one of the transition experiences was more successful than the other. The remaining chapters advocate the movement of Foundation Stage practice into Key Stage One, suggesting a principled approach to planning and a reflective approach to continuity and change. The final chapter recommends the improved expertise of teachers through critical reflection and action research.

What are the issues for children?

Getting the children's perspectives on issues of transition right

In order to find out how children feel about the experience of transition it is important to:

1. reflect on how we acquire that understanding, and
2. how we interpret what they tell us, and
3. how we represent the children's points of view.

There is an increasing awareness of the rights of children to participate in processes that might impact on their experiences. Article 12 of the United Nations Convention on the Rights of the Child (UN, 1989), states that children have a right to hold opinions about things that affect them. However, as White and Sharp (2007) point out, there is little evidence available concerning children's views of transition between Foundation Stage and Year One. They address this with their own research, the results of which will be considered within another chapter. An ethnographic approach, in which ample time is given to listen to and observe children in context, facilitates a move away from an adult-centred focus in order to seek a better understanding of the experiences in the setting from the children's perspective (Edmund, 2005). This is crucial, as teachers have values and priorities about children's needs that, even in an endeavour to get it right, may influence judgements about what children are telling us. I argue that what children say, do not say, do or do not do, is valuable information if gathered in sufficient time and over a period of time. How do we find out about children's feelings, expectations and anxieties? An obvious way to do this is to ask them directly. NFER research conducted by Sanders *et al.* (2005) used interviews with children that showed children valued the experiences of Reception Class and regretted the loss of opportunities to play when they moved to Year One. The children also did not like the requirement to sit and listen to the teacher. However, some children enjoyed the status of being in Year One and welcomed the challenges they would meet. This two-sided view of transition, that is, something to look forward to as a challenge and something to be anxious about was reflected in my own research. As adults we can surely identify with these mixed feelings of excitement and trepidation when entering a new phase such as a new job.

There may be a tendency to regard transition as a hurdle to be overcome in order to move on. This may be regarded as something difficult and a negative thing to happen. However, children often rise to and enjoy challenges and without perceived difficulties there would be less sense of accomplishment. Transition may also be regarded as a process or event that is 'done' to children, whereas children actively engage in 'constructing and reconstructing their own view of the world from their personal life experiences' (Fisher, 2009: 132).

I caution against the over-reliance on interviewing children as a means of determining the issues they have with transition. Westcott and Littleton (2005) offer an explanation for children's difficulty in responding to interviews. They say that children are more used to IRF discourse with adults. 'I' represents the initiating by the teacher, 'R' represents the child providing a response, and 'F' is the feedback from the teacher. Children are used to the type of interacting that happens in that setting, and will have clear ideas about what is expected of them. As the interview is a new type of interaction, it should be explained properly to the child. There is the danger that the child will provide the answers he/she feels is expected of them due to the power imbalance that inevitably exists between the child and the adult (Brooker, 2001; White and Sharp, 2007). To fully understand the issues involved in transition from Foundation Stage to Year One I argue that we should look further than asking the children for their points of view. We need to observe them in naturally occurring situations to improve our own understandings of what matters to them and how various aspects of practice impact on them. I strongly believe that we should take time to consider what they are telling us through what they are *not* saying or doing as well as what that say and do. A combined approach of seeking this information through interviews, observations and records will give a more authentic picture of the type of provision that suits the children and how they experience transition. A longitudinal ethnographic approach is suitable for the study of children, and enables the researcher to capture the 'critical transition periods that shape the processes of human development' (Buchbinder *et al.,* 2006). It also provides the space for the study of proximal processes (Bronfenbrenner, 1995) through children's naturally occurring experiences. This approach was used for the case studies that are explored within this book.

Discuss
- How could you find out from children how they really feel about the transition before, during and after the move from Reception Class to Year One?
- Does anyone ask them about their feelings?
- Are their feelings taken into consideration when planning?

Examples of brief interviews with children about their transition from Reception Class to Year One

The following brief conversations with children occurred in natural circumstances, for instance while having snack. They were part of a very informal interview approach in which the researcher wanted to prompt conversation about transition without asking too many probing questions; these may have led to answers the child thought the adult wanted to hear. For this reason they are brief. However, they do illustrate the difficulty in ascertaining what matters to children regarding transition to Key Stage One, and the reluctance to talk about it. However, they show that 'play' and 'work' feature in their thoughts about the move to Year One, and they show that each child has a different expectation of the transition.

Chris

This little boy was not really reluctant to talk in that he was not shy, but he would only say what he felt needed to be said. What seemed to be most important was that he already knew the teacher of Year One, as he had met her when in nursery. He spoke in a 'matter of fact' way about the things he felt he might do in the new phase. I do not think it showed indifference, but more that it was not something that concerned him.

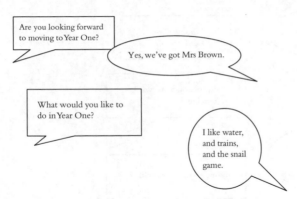

FIGURE 2.1   A conversation with Chris about moving to Year One

Neil

Neil was very confident about what he believed in. This came across in the interview when he had made up his mind that he would prefer to stay in Reception Class where he was sure that things were better. A better understanding of this developed during Year One when it became apparent that Neil worried about change and about not being certain where key people were going to be.

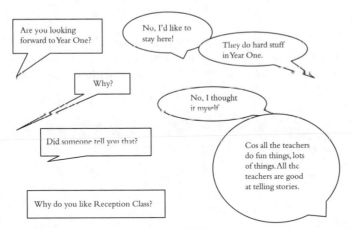

FIGURE 2.2   A conversation with Neil about moving to Year One

Gareth

Gareth enjoyed conversations and he opened up the interview with a statement about school. This precision about what he was saying and what he actually meant was typical of him. Gareth would make sure that you understood exactly what he was saying. However, as an interviewee, he would be in charge of the agenda and it was difficult to draw him away from this.

FIGURE 2.3   A conversation with Gareth about moving to Year One, which he initiated

James

James was reluctant to be interviewed, but drew a picture of what he liked in Reception Class, which was of boxes in the construction area. His only words were 'I like boxes'. He did not want to talk about moving to Year One. I think he did not want to know about it.

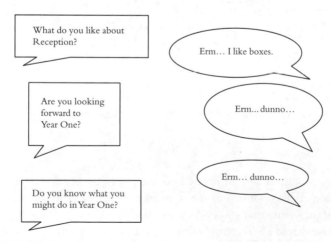

FIGURE 2.4   A conversation with James about moving to Year One

Christopher

It is not really clear why Christopher should associate the question about moving to Year One with fear and it may be a mistake to reach conclusions about this. I feel that he assumed that as adults were asking questions about it, there must be a reason to query how he felt.

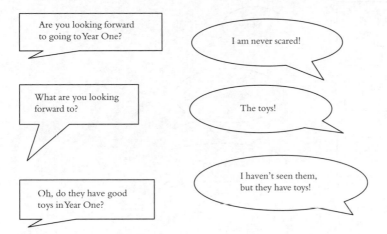

FIGURE 2.5   A conversation with Christopher about moving to Year One

Simon

Simon is a very able child who needed to be challenged academically and who had good social skills. He had no need to worry about perceived 'hard work' of Year One as expressed by one of his classmates. However, it was playing and friendship that were important to him

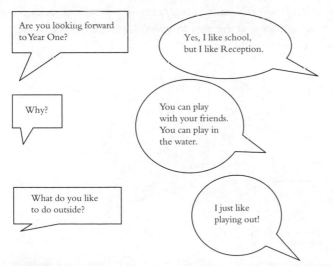

FIGURE 2.6   A conversation with Simon about moving to Year One

John

John had a very strong need to be outdoors. This had already been established, but was re-affirmed in this brief interview. He left no doubt as to what mattered to him when moving to Year One.

FIGURE 2.7   A conversation with John about moving to Year One

Luis

During this interview Luis drew a picture of a sand and water area that he enjoyed, but he did not want to talk about it. He was reluctant to enter into a conversation about the move to Year One. However, if we assume that the new footwear is for the new class, there must have been a conversation about this at home.

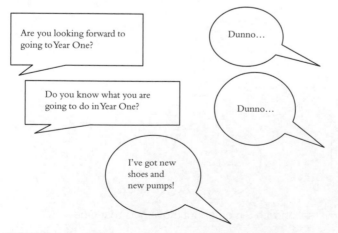

FIGURE 2.8   A conversation with Luis about moving to Year One

Discuss
- Do the children really know what to expect when they move to Year One?
- Do these children look forward to the move?
- If you were their teacher how would you reassure each of them?

What issues do children have with transition from Foundation Stage to Year One?

Generally speaking children look forward to the transition from Foundation Stage to Year One. This is because:

- they view it as a recognisable stage in 'growing up' and this gives them something to be proud of, and
- they are well informed about the process of transition and about what type of environment they are moving into
- preparation for transition has removed any mystery or misunderstandings they may have had
- they feel familiar with the new surrounding and new teachers and other practitioners.

The issues that arise are more likely to be due to a sudden change in practice, for which the children are unprepared and/or is unsuitable for some children's needs. It is broadly accepted that a shift to more formal, structured approaches creates difficulties for some children. This was an issue identified by teachers (Sanders *et al.*, 2005). This section will look more closely at this shift to a more formal approach, and attempt to identify the aspects that create difficulties for children. These aspects include:

- A need for autonomy.
- A need to articulate thoughts through play.
- A need to develop storytelling through play.
- A need to develop social skills and the ability to deal with conflict independently.
- To fulfil a desire to explore and investigate.
- To have uninterrupted thinking time.
- To fulfil a need to be outdoors.
- To have time away from adult supervision.

A need for autonomy

There are basic developmental needs children have, regardless of their wider experiences. From birth babies respond to stimuli and explore their immediate world. Haywood (2004) warns against the assumption that babies enter the world with a motive to explore, gain knowledge and mastery over it. He suggests that this tendency is shaped by important people in the child's life, initially parents and siblings and, later, teachers. Arguably, teachers should have a thorough understanding of the biology and psychology of child development. Henry (2004) explores the links between Darwin's basic tenet of evolution through natural selection and human development; that natural selection is the relationship, at every point, between an organism and its environment. This is not so much survival of the fittest: rather, satisfying the need for 'goodness of fit'. A small child constantly responds to stimuli with actions that may be reinforced as the child becomes able to replicate behaviours. The child will therefore develop in a way that enables him/her to be at one with the environment into which he/she is born and the environment in which he/she explores. This drive to explore and investigate does not cease at the end of the Foundation Stage. Teachers need to provide opportunities for the children to explore and investigate and make sense of this environment, and have an awareness of their role as part of that environment:

> In terms of human needs, satisfying the need for 'goodness-of-fit' empowers humans to meet the need to instigate a variety of actions, some of which are reinforced. Achieving greater freedom of action allows us to meet the need to discover and exchange new ideas leading to expanded insights.
>
> (Henry, 2004: 303)

The ability of the child to explore the environment will provide opportunities to deepen and consolidate understanding, therefore increasing insight into the environment, and enhancing the 'goodness-of-fit'. Further exploration and investigation will continue the process of expanding insight. The Plowden Report (CACE, 1967) advocated a child-centred approach in which individuals could learn through exploring and choosing within a carefully constructed environment. However, perhaps because of a lack of confidence in the certainty of outcomes of such an approach, education of young children in England reverted to more traditional, formal methods in which the adult has greater control over the agenda. Handing autonomy over to the children requires skilled support from adults who have a good understanding of child development and have the necessary skills and commitment to provide for individual needs within a structured environment.

Henry (2004) refers to Eriksson's (1950) three challenges for development, trust, autonomy and initiative, as fundamental developmental needs. She draws parallels with Dennett's (1995) evolutionary theory and Eriksson's (1950) phases of development. 'Trust' is when the child acquires a sense of goodness of fit with the environment; 'autonomy' is when the child begins to initiate his own action; 'initiative' is using the brain to give and gain insights about the environment (Henry, 2004: 304). If this theory is sound then teachers need to consider their role in enabling children to have first hand experiences in the physical environment, to have a sense of 'goodness-of-fit', and they should encourage autonomy. The use of interaction between adult/child and child/child and the environment will enable the child to use initiative and gain more insight.

Claxton (2002) believes that we can build learning power, and identifies four characteristics that can be fostered in order to achieve this: resilience, resourcefulness, reflectiveness and reciprocity. The teacher can support children in developing these characteristics to become autonomous learners. Giving children study skills, tips and techniques may support learning, but does prompt the question: are we providing children with fixed structures that they learn to perform within, and in doing so restrict creativity and ingenuity? Perhaps we should be developing their individual learning capacities by 'coaching' them (Claxton, 2002). The latter need not exclude the teaching of skills and techniques, or information giving, but a shift in emphasis might prevent the restriction of creativity. I would argue that teachers of Foundation Stage, Key Stage One and beyond have a responsibility to enable children to become autonomous learners so that they can continue to find 'goodness of fit' in a rapidly changing world.

Providing opportunities for, and fostering autonomy, is closely linked with motivation:

> Intrinsically motivated persons work harder, persist longer in tasks, prefer self-regulation over externally imposed regulation, set 'leaner' schedules of reinforcement for themselves, prefer novel, difficult, and complex tasks, and are more likely to pursue new learning on their own.
>
> (Haywood, 2004: 236)

I caution against an assumption that open access to play will provide opportunities for autonomy without barriers. I generally would argue that it is through freedom, choice and autonomy in play that children are most able to interact with the environment, and fulfil a basic need for 'goodness-of-fit'. However, Campbell (2005) says that choice is not just about freedom from adult control, as there are other barriers to overcome such as gender. This notion creates a dilemma for practitioners who want to give freedom and choice, and in Campbell's study practitioners were intervening to support children's rights to play anywhere. The tension between freedom and autonomy through play and the interactions within play limiting choice were examined by Ryan (2005) who found that gender was a key factor in exercising power in play. She found that boys generally used physical strategies to exercise power, and girls were good at creating stories that enabled them to enter into other children's play. She was left wondering if free play enabled differences to be confirmed and embedded.

It is not just gender issues that create obstacles to freedom and choice for children. Adult values about other aspects of life, which may be cultural, can also be transferred through play. Lofdahl's (2006) study of a Swedish pre-school found that children used the content of their play to get a superior status position. An example of this was the distribution of props in role play, in which the children chose dressing-up clothes that represented a lead role in the play. The possession of a crown represented superiority. This was reinforced by language that confirmed the status of the child in possession of the relevant item. The adult may have a part to play in restricting the freedom and autonomy of some individuals in order to allow that of others.

Case study example

By the end of the nursery phase I concluded that Neil had aspects of character that seemed to oppose each other. He could socialise yet often chose to be alone. He was often reluctant to take part in group activities; he was independent yet sometimes needed to be reassured and, although assertive, showed sensitivity and a sense of what was fair. These characteristics were still generally evident throughout the Reception Class year. He showed sensitivity towards other children, for example he would sit for long periods with a partner at the computer letting the partner take the lead when playing computer games. This was not due

15

to lack of interest or ability, as when the partner would eventually move away Neil would take over the controls and skilfully and enthusiastically continue. His equal satisfaction between working with others and playing alone also continued. He enjoyed the indoor and outdoor environments apparently in equal measure.

Year One Class was mostly adult-led with opportunities to play mostly in the afternoon, and very limited access to the outdoors. Neil appeared to be less engaged in Year One Class. The more formal, taught inputs on the carpet did not seem to inspire him. For instance, one observation showed that throughout a whole interactive story session with a tape and costumes for children to take roles and undertake actions, Neil stared around the room. When called by teacher to take part, he momentarily copied her 'actions'. Often when the teacher asked for volunteers to do tasks for her, such as preparing something for a display, there was no response from Neil. He did not appear to have a need to please the adult. It seems that it was not the nature of the adult-led activity that was problematic, as this was interactive and engaged most of the children. For Neil, it was a strong desire for autonomy that was not being provided for to the same extent in this new phase, which created difficulties for him. This desire for autonomy applied to group situations as well as solitary activity.

Discuss
- What were the differences between Foundation Stage and Year One?
- What does Neil need to make him happy and make progress in Year One?
- How could the teacher incorporate his need for autonomy into planning?

A need to articulate thoughts through play

Speech is an important cultural tool in transforming knowledge within the school. It is an important tool with which a child interacts with the environment (physical, cultural and human), and therefore has an effect on experiences in the school. There are obvious differences between the dialogue that occurs during adult–initiated planned sessions and those that occur through play. Research commissioned by Sure Start showed that practitioners 'often close down language opportunities, take over children's conversation, leave what children have to say unheard, and force children to attend to narrow, overprescribed notions of what is good communication and language' (Ellis, 2005: 12, 13).

The recommendations resulting from this research emphasise the need for listening before talking to children. They include the recommendation that practitioners should be comfortable with children's silences, allowing them time to think and to consider a response. Katz (2004) emphasised the need for conversations with children in which the response was contingent with the child's comments. Ellis (2005) states that questioning needs to be done carefully so that it does not resemble interrogation. Purposeful activity leads to better learning, and it should also lead to 'richer language than might occur in artificially created situations' (Ellis, 2005: 12, 13). The combination of experience and language are perhaps basic essentials for the learning process to occur.

The nature of the involvement of adults working with children, sharing activities and using language to expand insight will affect the quality of the child's learning experience. It is what the Effective Provision of Pre-school Education (EPPE) project calls 'sustained shared thinking', and defines it as:

> An episode in which two or more individuals 'work together' in an intellectual way to solve a problem, clarify a concept, evaluate activities, extend a narrative etc. Both parties must contribute to the thinking and it must develop and extend.
>
> (Siraj-Blatchford *et al.*, 2003: 6)

For this to happen effectively adults must allow the child time to think, and must listen and make appropriate responses. The activity should be meaningful and the adult should not dominate the discourse (Ellis, 2005). The concept of 'sustained shared thinking' is included in the standards for Early Years Professional Status but, in my experience, is widely misunderstood. In some ways drawings allow the child to continue to work on their thoughts and make alterations, unlike the spoken utterance, which, once said, is complete. Provision of appropriate materials, within the areas in which children play, enable children to do this and can be a platform for the child to articulate those thoughts when they feel ready.

Case study example

Gareth did not need to be coaxed into a conversation. In Reception Class he showed an ability to empathise and be sensitive to how a child might respond to what he said. An example of this is when he asked a child not to stand on a spider because 'he won't hurt you'. He complimented other children in an adult fashion, for instance when he wanted to copy a design for a card he said 'Where did you get that idea from, it's great?' Gareth showed curiosity about many things, but seemed to be particularly interested in what people were doing and saying. He almost always talked when involved in activities, whether they were child-initiated or adult-led. Gareth went into great detail about a barbeque they had had at home. He used complex sentences, adding supplementary information. For instance, he told the group that they had a barbeque, and added that 'you must say BBQ, not barbeque, because if you say "barbeque", it will rain, my brother said so'. When talking about the barbeque at his house, he added the name of the road in the sentence. He also responded well to adults' questions or comments. He spent a considerable amount of time outdoors where he negotiated with friends to compile a set of rules for an invented game. He also spent time alone in the construction area outdoors, drawing, then would wander over to his teacher and use his drawing to initiate a conversation.

Year One Class was mostly adult-led with few opportunities to play, usually in the afternoon and with very limited access to the outdoors. Observations of Gareth during Year One were of a subdued child, who teachers referred to as often being sullen. This was despite the fact that he said he preferred to do 'real work' and 'hard work'. This was a complete contrast from the observations made during Reception Class, when he had been animated retelling and developing a story, and articulating his thoughts with adults and children during play.

Discuss

- What were the reasons for Gareth's apparent unhappiness in Year One?
- How could the teacher improve Gareth's experience?
- Why did Reception Class provide a happier experience for him?

Case study example

During the Foundation Stage it was evident that Chris was friendly, happy and enjoyed playing. He was confident with adults and invited them enthusiastically into his play. He was much more likely to engage in conversations with adults during play than in adult-initiated carpet inputs. He enjoyed playing in the construction area, where he was creative and played collaboratively, developing a story as he played. Chris's grasp of numbers developed during Reception Year. He could order numbers and understood the relevance of the 'last number in the count' representing a given total. He liked to talk about his calculations. The Year One Class was formal and mostly adult-led. The adjacent area of resources was seldom used and access to outdoors was very limited. In Year One Chris seemed able to sit for long periods on the carpet for the teacher input, but often appeared not to have grasped the concept that had been introduced. He managed to complete straightforward sums despite the lack of number lines or counters to support the task. However, if the way the sum was set out changed, he struggled. He did not have opportunities to talk about his mathematics activities and was not ready to use recorded methods. He was heard saying 'this is boring' in reference to written mathematics tasks. During this year, Chris did not appear to be unhappy, but was less enthusiastic for his tasks.

Discuss

- What are the links between articulating thought and learning new concepts?
- How might Chris's experiences have been improved in Year One?

A need to develop storytelling through play

According to the National Primary Strategy's 'Talk for Writing' programme (DfCSF, 2008), effective writers have an ongoing internal dialogue that shapes their writing and children need this process made explicit through talk. Role play is one area that provides opportunities for children to develop their stories. This can be done through solitary play when a child is involved in make-belief, sometimes talking to themselves. Children can be heard negotiating over roles during collaborative play and their dialogue reveals the sharing of thoughts about the development of the story they are dramatising. This is surely a vital process for children to engage in if they are to develop the skills of storytelling, and writing stories for others to read. The space for this to occur through play enables the children to explore the language that conveys their ideas to others. Their peers act like critical friends who will ask for clarification or dispute decisions, compelling the child to review their story ideas and consider how they articulate it to others.

Information and communications technology (ICT) can be used by the children to develop stories. For example, 2simple software produced 2Create a Story, which enables children to work independently or with friends to create a story that can be recorded in picture, sound and movement. Digital photographs taken by children can be used to tell and retell stories. Photographs taken during short journeys or activities can be used to play back in sequence to support the retelling of stories and can also be used to create books to which the children can add text when they are ready.

Storytelling is not just important for the development of the spoken and written language. The freedom to develop stories through play supports creative development. I identify five areas for adult's consideration when planning to provide such opportunities:

- Inspiration, which can be provided through pictures, experiences, sounds and music, and various resources.
- Appreciation, in which adults show that they value the stories created by the children.
- Expressions, as children should have the freedom to express their own ideas in their own way.
- Emotions, which can be expressed through the stories being created, and can be enhanced with the use of music. Children often use stories to work through issues they have.
- Imagination, which will grow if children are given time and space to explore, ponder and invent.

Case study example

George, Nicholas, David and Thomas arrived in Reception Class one morning and began talking while other children were arriving. They competed for attention when talking about events that had happened the previous day. George began to tell the story of a police incident he had witnessed the previous evening. He described how he had seen a police car, then another arrived, and that the 'baddy' was hiding in some bushes. He was quite animated and showed considerable awareness of his audience. His friends started to join in and wanted to elaborate on the story, which frustrated George who was adamant about what had actually happened. The children began to re-enact the story moving into a reading corner, negotiating who was taking the roles and what pieces of furniture represented the environment of the story setting. I was just relishing in the wonderful opportunity I had to observe this, when the story was brought to an abrupt halt by the teacher for register time. I felt the disappointment that showed on the children's faces.

Discuss
- Should the children have opportunities to develop stories through play in Year One?
- How can this be achieved and how would you know that this was having a positive impact on their language development, storytelling and story writing?
- How might the development of story through play and use of digital photography prepare children to use writing frames?
- Is play a vital component of developing the ability to create stories?

A need to develop social skills and the ability to deal with conflict independently

'Children who are encouraged to feel free to express their ideas and their feelings, such as joy, sadness, frustration and fear, can develop strategies to cope with new, challenging or stressful situations' (DCSF, 2008). The Social and Emotional Aspects of Learning (SEAL) materials were based on evidence from the United States of the impact of social and emotional learning on school achievement. They were written by teams of psychologists and focused on aspects such as understanding and managing feelings, empathy, friendship, belonging, resolving conflicts and so on (DfES, 2005). This aspect of learning is one that should be given adequate attention for its impact on the quality of daily life of the children, and for its impact on all other aspects of learning.

Case study example

James did not talk very much in Reception Class, except for small interchanges between himself and another child during play. During group time, when the passing around of a toy indicated his turn to talk, he shook his head to indicate that he did not wish to speak. At snack time he was surrounded by children talking but would sit quietly. The report confirmed what had been observed in that James was reluctant to talk in group situations. He was observed engaging in short, quiet conversations with children adjacent to him when playing in the construction area. He tended to flit between the different areas, including between the indoors and outdoors.

James was reluctant to be interviewed, but drew a picture of what he liked in Reception Class, which was of boxes in the construction area. His only words were 'I like boxes'. Year One Class was mostly adult-led with opportunities to play mostly in the afternoon, and very limited access to the outdoors. In Year One James was still very reluctant to be interviewed; it was difficult even to get one-word answers out of him. He was obedient during teacher-led activities, but struggled to concentrate after short periods. He preferred to play and was frequently reprimanded for running and pushing other children. The adult always dealt with the conflict that resulted from this. When involved in tasks, he was easily distracted. If his friends moved on he would follow even if he had not completed a set task. His natural ability was not a cause for concern, but his immaturity meant that he needed help to keep focused in order to make progress. He did not respond to adult-initiated activity and, if adults had wanted to develop his verbal interaction with them, they would need to approach this very sensitively through play.

Discuss
- What does James need to support his social development in Year One?
- How might the teacher encourage his social interaction?
- How should planning take account of his needs?

Case study example

Although Simon was gentle in nature, never showing aggression, he was able to stand up for himself and showed remarkable ability, for his age, in solving conflicts. If he felt that there was an injustice, such as a toy being taken from him, he would clearly explain the circumstances to an adult. On one occasion when such an incident had occurred, he was given the disputed tricycle for a first go by the adult. However, after a few minutes, he ran over to the other child and said 'Do you want a go?' His friend John was also in dispute over a tricycle with another child. The teacher persuaded him to take on another role, handing him a traffic patrol outfit and sign. He appeared to conform, but after a short period he used his 'authority' as a traffic patrol officer, raising his hand to halt the progress of the tricycle in question. This resulted in the repossession of the tricycle.

Discuss
- Is it possible to enable children to develop skills in dealing with conflict if there is a formal approach in which adults control the learning activities?
- What is your policy on dealing with conflict amongst children?
- Are colleagues aware of their responsibilities to support children in learning to deal with conflict?

To fulfil a desire to explore and investigate

The need for a child to have autonomy has been discussed earlier in this chapter. Autonomy is essential if a child is to explore and investigate. However, freedom to explore does not necessarily mean that it is a solitary activity. Bronfenbrenner (1995) believes that child development occurs through a process of progressively more complex interaction between the active child and people, objects and symbols in the immediate environment. Exploration and investigation is of the whole environment including the people, as well as the physical surroundings and the cultural tools that it comprises. 'It is important to consider the contexts in which children are developing their conceptualisations, the socio-culturally relevant activities within those contexts, and the participation with guidance and support of others' (Robbins, 2005: 6).

Case study example

Christopher was a friendly child in Reception Class. His Foundation Stage Report commented on how he always arrived to school with a smile and had good relationships. He enjoyed having responsibility, such as taking the register to the office. He could help himself to snacks and use the self-registering system when choosing tasks. He would use fingers to join in calculations and joined in rhymes and refrains. He enjoyed the 'small world' area, and showed a preference for construction. When in the construction area, he would spend considerable time trying out different things such as using nuts and bolts with a tool. He estimated length during such activities, could use rotating parts and showed a strong awareness of symmetry. On one occasion, he produced an intricate construction that he said was the inside of a clock; he had been trying to dismantle a clock earlier in the day. Christopher was happy playing on his own and equally happy when playing with a group of children. He was very comfortable talking with both his peers and adults. His Foundation Stage Report said that he was inquisitive and used knowledge he gained to design models. He spent much of the time allocated for access to the outdoors, outside.

The Year One Class had some provision for children to consolidate learning through play, but access to this and the outdoors was limited. There was much less evidence of the confidence and enthusiasm in Year One. There was more time spent on the carpet with the teacher, and less practical or interactive involvement. Much of the mathematics activities observed were carpet input time and worksheets. He always grasped new mathematical concepts very quickly, and could have been challenged more. His curiosity was less evident in this class. It is not possible to state if Christopher's enthusiasm for construction or outdoor activities remained from the previous year as neither was available to the children during visits. Although there seemed to be more teaching Christopher showed less enthusiasm, and there was much less evidence of progress in Year One.

Discuss
- What does Christopher need to make him happy and make progress in Year One?
- Does your provision enable children to spend time exploring and investigating the environment?

To have uninterrupted thinking time

It is important for children to have time for uninterrupted thought processes in which they embed concepts. The chunking of time to suit adult planning can mean there is insufficient time in an episode of play for depth in thought and embedding of concepts (May *et al.*, 2006). It is a difficult task for teachers to organise a day and orchestrate activities in such a way as to ensure they have provided adequate time for a) adult-led learning activities for groups and individuals, b) individual support and c) uninterrupted periods of play. Interruptions to play often frustrate children. This should not be difficult for adults to understand as we can feel frustrated if we are interrupted when engaged in a task that requires our concentration. The difficulties in providing a balance are perhaps a reason why some teachers choose a more formal approach. There would be fewer frustrating interruptions to play. Therefore the teacher needs to value play in order to justify the time and effort required to provide it.

Case study example

Simon played collaboratively in Reception Class and Year One, often investigating in water and sand, articulating his thoughts, and was able to negotiate. He was very good at taking turns and encouraging others to 'have a go'. Simon showed an ability to remain on task for significant periods when involved in adult-directed activity and quickly developed strategies to write independently, using knowledge of phonics, recall and words in the environment. The attention he gave to a task was remarkable and usually the tasks were reasonably challenging. Simon was able to work in partnership with other children, sharing the activity and sharing thought and tended to be above average in terms of success in most curriculum areas. This was confirmed by his class records. He could often be seen engaged in an activity available in continuous provision, which was meant to help children consolidate their learning; it was apparent that he was repeating and making sense of learning from an adult-led input. There were occasions, however, when Simon was prevented from remaining on self-chosen activities because of interruptions due to timetabling. This was usually because the teacher was withdrawing groups of children from free play to have a focused session with her. On occasions he showed a facial expression indicating resignation and was sometimes heard saying 'Oh no, we've only just started!' or 'Oh no! Why do we have to tidy up when we've only just started!' Such interruptions appeared to be the greatest cause of dissatisfaction for Simon.

Case study example

Ben showed persistence and keen interest when engaged in self-chosen activity. Sometimes this would involve a sedentary task. For example, in the sand tray he would spend up to half an hour smoothing the surface of a bucket of sand, examining it closely, his concentration being seemingly unaffected by noisy and boisterous activity in the vicinity. Also when involved in chasing and teasing other children, he would keep returning to the same activity, similarly after enforced interruptions, such as snack time. Ben's enthusiasm for sand continued to the end of Reception Class. He would spend long periods of time investigating the properties of sand, in particular, the movement of sand through tubes and funnels. He would repeatedly stop and restart the flow of sand through such contraptions, and talk about what was happening to other children. He also frequently chose water and construction for play. Neither was available for most of the time in Year One.

Discuss
- How can teachers provide a balance between adult-initiated and child-initiated activity without causing abrupt interruptions?
- How do interruptions impact on learning?
- How could you avoid interrupting children when they are engrossed in their investigations?

To fulfil a need to be outdoors

There are arguments for improving access to the outdoors for educational reasons that are not discussed here. This focus is on biophilia, in which the child has a natural need to be outdoors. We should not undervalue the additional benefits of improving children's well-

FIGURE 2.9   A *need* to be outdoors

being, both emotionally and physically, through continuous access to the outdoors. The outdoor space is sometimes larger than the indoor space and therefore offers opportunities for children to have a little time alone exploring, imagining and pondering (Harding, 2005). The outdoor environment, and especially one that is natural such as a forest school, provides greater opportunities for risk taking; this especially so for physical activity. Waters and Begley (2007) suggest that this is because adults do not just allow it, they provide for risk taking outdoors. They observed children indoors and outdoors, finding that the children were much more likely to take risks outdoors, and were also less likely to be reprimanded for non-compliant behaviour. They saw excitement in children outdoors that had not been observed indoors. If children have space and permission to move and explore, they can take risks and find out about themselves without fear of being admonished for boisterous, noisy behaviour (Ouvry, 2003). Jarvis (2007) found that boys' play tended to be of a high energy level compared with that of girls; this was particularly so when there was 'boys only' play. The outdoors provides the space for this energy to be expended.

Case study example

John took every opportunity to be outdoors and told me that this was the best thing at school. His eagerness was very evident when asked why he liked to go outdoors. He said, 'there are bikes and no roof. It's lighter, better than inside. When indoors, if he heard the keys for the door to the outdoor provision rattle, he appeared almost instantaneously, waiting to get through the door. When outdoors, he seemed much more alert and had very good motor skills. For example, one day when other children struggled to retrieve a ball from a tight corner, he skilfully got it using his foot. He also seemed to be interested in anything that moved. As well as playing with wheels and balls, he spent some time watching closely how these move. John knew why he wanted to be outdoors. It offered him a sense of freedom with 'no roof'. Although recognised as an intelligent child with remarkable general knowledge, he struggled to concentrate and to follow more than one instruction. His space to move outdoors freed him from the constraints of tasks he was finding difficult to focus on. In Year One there was no access to the outdoors other than regular school breaks.

To have time away from adult supervision

Children like to have 'secret places' or dens in which they can have experiences alone or with friends, away from the view of adults. Kylin (2003) found that children talk about the secret places or dens in terms of what they do there, such as playing games, whereas adults tend to talk about the physical structure and aesthetics. Any corner out of the immediate sight of adults can be considered as a den. Often these are outdoors and frequently demarcated by simple objects, such as a couple of twigs. They are often close to adults, but out of sight. Barnard (2006) says that outdoor spaces are becoming increasingly limited in what they offer because of fear of litigation, and the increased availability of electronic media lures children indoors. A possible factor is parents' fear of letting children out alone and their desire to keep a watchful eye on their children. Children need space to discover themselves, but with reduced provision for autonomy and reduced access to the outdoors often associated with a move to Year One, there may be a risk that children do not have this time.

Case study example

Luis was confident and mixed well with children. However, his timidity was apparent on occasions when attention was turned to him in large group or whole class situations, evidenced by uncertain expressions, such as his finger in his mouth and tongue movements. Although he would often spontaneously follow groups of children running excitedly, there were occasions when he would take a lead and make up the rules of the game. He often used aggressive faces when playing, for example when crashing his car deliberately into the vehicle of another child and pushing others in wheeled toys so fast that they objected. This was in contrast with the more timid behaviour he showed when in the presence of adults. Much of his child-initiated play was outdoors. When required to do adult-initiated tasks he was compliant and would remain on task as long as was required of him, but was subdued.

The Year One Class was formal and mostly adult-led. The adjacent area of resources was seldom used and there was very limited access to the outdoors. In Year One, Luis remained confident with other children and was willing but not eager to talk with adults. He showed a remarkable ability to keep focused during adult-led activity, at the start of this year.

So what are the children telling us about their needs for transition to Year One?

There are some general conclusions that most practitioners would reach that are unsurprising:

- The children know what they like.
- The children know what is important to them.
- The children know they are moving to a new phase.
- The children do not display anxiety about the prospect of moving to a new phase.
- The children like to play.

What is noticeable is that the needs of the children are varied, and that a 'one size fits all' approach is not appropriate.

For many children this is a positive thing as it is a demarcation of phases, and they celebrate moving 'up' to the next phase, and being at 'big school'. Sanders *et al.* (2005) found that the younger/less mature children and those with special needs encountered most difficulties. Children's views revealed that they were unhappy with the loss of opportunities to learn through play, and they valued their experiences in Reception Class. They were worried about the amount of writing expected in Year One, and about having to sit still. This is in keeping with White and Sharp's (2007) research in which it was found that children liked the idea of growing up or getting bigger but worried about hard work. They suggest that children develop the link between writing tasks and 'work' while in Reception Class and worry that there is more of this in Year One as 'hard work' is linked to growing up. I found evidence of this view being promoted by several parents.

Children identified as having special educational needs

The brief interviews above demonstrated that each child has different perspectives on transition to the new phase and it was then demonstrated that each child has his own needs before, during and after transition. Children who have been identified as having special educational needs will, similarly, have their own perspectives and needs on transition to the new phase. However, it might be argued that these are likely to be more profound. Below are the stories of two children with identified special educational needs and their experiences during the transition between Foundation Stage and Key Stage One. They are not representative of all the possible issues related to special needs, but highlight the need to be aware of more profound needs.

Niall

Context

Niall joined Reception Class after spending the previous year in a nearby maintained nursery. The Reception Class had an experienced teacher who had a balance of adult-led activity and child-initiated activity. There was also a part-time classroom assistant who was sensitive and intuitive in the way she interacted with the children. Adults were sometimes invited into children's play and used this to learn more about the children and subtly support their learning and development. The class was fortunate to have an experienced nursery nurse each morning who was often drawn into children's play; she seemed to instinctively know how to become involved in the play, support learning yet not interfere with the children's direction. The class teacher valued play and valued subtle support of learning and development through play. There were short, whole class activities on the carpeted area that were interactive. Individuals and groups of children were often selected for focused work with the teacher. The teacher and assistant were aware of the children's reluctance to be removed from their play for such work and tried to organise this so that they began the task before children went to play. However, there were some signs of frustration from children who were called to the task from their play.

Niall's story

At the start of the school year it was immediately realised that Niall had difficulties with the classroom routines and expectations of behaviour. Although there were no records sent to the school about any concerns, his difficulties were serious. He would not join in any collaborative games or play. At Christmas time he showed no interest in decorating the tree with the rest of the class. He seemed to be totally uninterested in the activities that the other children enjoyed, such as baking. He swore quite badly and behaved inappropriately with women staff, for instance, looking up their skirts. He seemed to wander around the class knocking anything in his path out of the way, including other children. He did not show any interest in other people at all and it was difficult to get eye contact with him. There was, however, a noticeable exception to this, in that he showed affection for one of his peers who had learning difficulties.

Despite the relatively informal approach of this Reception Class, it did not seem possible to engage Niall in a way that would support his progress. He also caused significant disruption indoors and his peers felt intimidated by the physical behaviour described above. An educational psychologist was called very early on and diagnosed Asperger's syndrome, but a very rare aspect of it that was quite profound. In addition to this, Niall had medication for epilepsy, which on occasions subdued him; on these days he was not disruptive but it concerned the teacher that he did not appear to gain anything from being in the class.

Due to the severity of Niall's difficulties a full-time assistant, Doris, was appointed to work with him. Doris was patient, kind and prepared to try various strategies to engage him. She was successful in doing things with him and found that he needed to wander and explore. The indoor and outdoor environment of this Reception Class allowed this to happen and, because of the one-to-one support, Niall could move freely without risk to other children. Although he seemed to be unaware of other children, those who knew him recognised that he was aware of them and what they were doing, but he chose not to take part. It remained impossible to coax him into joining in with other children, or to be directed by an adult. There was more sustained attention to tasks that were self-chosen. There was a continuing anxiety felt by the teacher about whether or not his needs were being met, but overall he was happy and cared for.

Niall's move to Year One

The close proximity of the Year One classroom to Reception Class and the shared entrance, in addition to the ongoing employment of Doris, meant that there was some familiarity and continuity for Niall as he moved into Year One. However, there was a complete contrast in the practice. As the children entered the room at 9am they went straight to their designated chair at a table and would spend a significant amount of time at this place. Niall was not expected to do this; he had Doris who carefully planned each day for him and who would follow his interests and desires. An observer might have concluded that Niall was happy and cared for and making progress at his own rate. Unfortunately, having observed Niall during Reception Class and Year One I noticed a worrying trend. He spent the majority of his time outside of the classroom because a) there was less space for movement in class and b) the formal teacher-led focus for large parts of the day prevented Niall's involvement (he would have distracted the children who were listening to the teacher). Therefore Niall spent little time in the classroom, did not take part in assemblies, physical education (PE lessons or any other collaborative exercises. Other than his companion, Doris, he had a more solitary existence. He seldom had access to the one child he did seem to relate to, the child with learning difficulties, as that child was able to cope with the Year One routines.

Before the end of Year One, Niall was removed from school to await a place in a special school.

Discuss
- What type of provision would best suit Niall's needs?
- Were his needs met in Reception Class?
- How might this have been improved?
- Why was inclusion so difficult in Year One?
- Could his needs have been better provided for at the school?

Elliot

Context

Elliot had recently moved into the area when he joined Reception Class at the start of the school year. His birthday was in the summer months. He enjoyed most of the experiences available to him in an environment that valued free movement and play as a substantial part of the provision. However, he struggled as his activity became more controlled by adults. For instance, despite the interactive nature of the whole class story or singing sessions (which were of appropriate duration for most of the children), he seemed unable to remain in one place.

Elliot's story

For much of the time he played freely, and coped with short one-to-one sessions. He did, however, have difficulties in sharing resources with other children. He would become very aggressive with his classmates and if an adult had to intervene he became more aggressive.

Sometimes this would result in violent behaviour, for instance throwing chairs across the room. At other times he would hide under a table and refuse to come out.

Elliot's parents had separated before the move to the new area and he now lived with his mother and her partner. His mother and partner often brought him to school, frequently discussed his needs with the teacher and were keen to work in partnership to improve Elliot's behaviour and experiences. There was also a good level of support from a grandmother who was firm but affectionate with him. The dialogue between the parents and staff, most often on a daily basis when delivering him to or collecting him from school, was very important in monitoring his progress and trying to understand his difficulties. One particular event provided some information about what may have contributed to his problems. He was outdoors at an easel, painting. The teacher happened to be close by when he seemed to complete a well formed picture of house with a roof, windows and other features. He continued to paint lines across the windows and then began to almost obliterate the features of his painting. In a bid to 'rescue' the work, the teacher halted the activity and he was asked why he had 'spoiled' his painting. He said that it was his old house and that the windows were smashed because his dad had done it when he was 'mad', and the rest of the house had been 'trashed'. Subsequent conversations with his mother revealed a difficult relationship, which had ongoing access issues.

The teacher and classroom assistants were very understanding and agreed strategies for supporting Elliot, which included avoidance of situations that were known to trigger his aggression. The ongoing partnership between school and family enabled improvements, but there were still regular episodes of aggression during free play and adult–directed group tasks. He was eventually diagnosed as having Attention Deficit Disorder and was given Ritalin. This caused anxiety because the adults in the classroom expressed concerns about the use of a drug to deal with the problem, but admitted a sense of relief (and guilt) when his symptoms were subdued.

Part-time assistance was provided to support Elliot. He made progress and there were fewer incidents, possibly because the adults had developed an understanding and adjusted their expectations. He was able to move freely, and yet gradually was getting used to the idea of conformity with some of the school routines.

Elliot's move to Year One

The Year One Class teacher met with the Reception teacher and classroom assistant to discuss Elliot's needs before the transition to Year One. The management of the school decided to transfer the assistant to Year One Class at the same time; this provided more informed knowledge about the children, including Elliot. The difficulties experienced by Elliot did not change during Year One. However, the awareness of his difficulties grew because a) there was a more formal approach to Year One and b) he was more likely to be expected to take part in whole school functions, for instance assemblies. It was the nature and duration of each of these that presented difficulties. Often he spent time with an adult outside the main classroom area doing tasks. Sadly, he was labelled as a 'difficult' child and due to the organisation of the school he encountered more adults, some of whom did not understand his problems. These encounters were more likely to result in aggressive behaviour. Although the culture of the school was one that fostered parental partnerships, the more formal approach at the start and end of the day in Year One did not facilitate an ongoing dialogue. Instead, meetings were arranged in response to particular events.

Discuss

- Was Reception Class provision suited to Elliot's needs?
- How might this have been improved?
- Why were there apparently more episodes of difficult behaviour in Year One?
- Should the Reception Class and Year One Class teachers have done more to prepare for Elliot's transition?
- How would you deal with the dilemma of meeting a child's needs and supporting him in coping with conformity?
- Is it a teacher's responsibility to prepare children for an increasingly formal approach as children move through the key stages?

Key messages

- Children are affected by transition and changes in practice in different ways.
- Children are not happy to lose opportunities to play when they join Year One.
- Children view transition to the next phase as a positive thing marking their 'growing up'.
- Children with special needs and younger children encounter most difficulties in transition to Year One.

What are the issues for parents and practitioners?

Chapter content

The chapter begins by looking at the issues of transition to Key Stage One for parents. It then uses three case study schools, High Bank School, Park Green School and Meadow Lane School, to examine teachers' perspectives on transition issues.

What are the issues about transition for parents?

Dockett *et al.* (1999) studied the views of parents and educators about what is important about children's transition to school. They found that the majority of parents and educators wanted children to be happy, feel positive, and settle into school routines easily. However, they discovered that the experiences that were part of the transition were 'multi dimensional', and that different children experience the same process in different ways as they make adjustments to different people, routines and contexts. They suggest that the geographic context is a key factor that affects the transition experience, but that the ways people respond to the issues of transition varied within geographical locations. Factors affecting this might include the length of time and mode of travel to the setting, or the distance between the locations of the pre-school and Key Stage One building, or even the nature of the layout and organisation. Other factors might include the variety of pre-school settings the children have attended before entering the school setting, resulting in the children and families not being familiar with each other. They concluded that successful transition programmes would look quite different, as they would be responding to the local community needs.

Parental attitudes will have an impact on how children respond to the anticipation of and process of transition to the new phase. Common sense dictates that if parents show anxiety then children will also feel anxious. An important issue for parents is the desire to have more information about the transition (Sanders *et al.*, 2005). The parents want to know what will be expected of the children so that they can prepare them for this. They also want to meet the Year One teacher before the new academic year commences. This lack of involvement with parents had also been identified as a key issue by IFF research (IFF, 2004).

The NFER research also found that there was a strongly expressed desire for training for Key Stage One teachers in how to provide for the transition from the Foundation Stage (Sanders *et al.*, 2005). This research found that the biggest challenge identified by teachers was the move from a play-based curriculum to a more structured approach. The introduction to the literacy and numeracy lessons was cited as an example of a problem in that it was difficult to get children to sit and listen to the adult. The ability to sit still and listen to the teacher was identified by school staff as a key skill needed by children if they were to make a good start in Year One. IFF (2004) found that the Early Years practitioners were unsure of the outcomes of the transition process.

Discuss
- What are the parental concerns regarding transition to Year One?
- What reassurance could be provided?

Issues identified by teachers in three case study settings

In each of these case study schools, there was movement of teachers between the Foundation Stage and Key Stage One and there was satisfaction with the quality of the preparation of the children for transition. However, the interviews with teachers revealed that there were marked differences in their experiences.

High Bank School

The staff at this school felt that one of the most positive aspects of transition was that the staff moved between phases and between the children centre and the school. For instance, one teacher had worked in the birth to three unit, the nursery and in Year One. Therefore there were no concerns about teacher ability to work across the phases, or their own transition between them. They were all satisfied with the preparation meetings they had with parents and children before transition to Year One. In keeping with the findings of the NFER research, teachers expressed concerns for particular children who were young and children who were struggling with some aspects of learning. They felt that the more formal approach of Year One would not suit these children. Other issues that concerned them were in relation to expectations of staff in Key Stage One as follows:

- Teachers and teaching assistants in Reception Class spent a considerable amount of time over a two-week period, collecting and assembling assessment data that had been demanded of them by managers in Key Stage One. This was in addition to the Foundation Stage Profiles. During this time the children were involved in free play with little attention being given to supporting their needs. The teachers lamented the fact that they had neglected the children in order to comply with the requirement to complete new assessment records.
- Year One teachers admitted that they did not use the Foundation Stage Profiles to plan for the needs of the children. The reason was that the Key Stage One manager insisted that they used the assessment data required by Key Stage One managers for planning, instead of the Foundation Stage Profiles.

- Year One teachers felt unable to provide activities that they believed were suited to children being introduced to Year One because of the pressures to take part in timetabled activities that fitted in with Key Stage One and the rest of the school.

Park Green School

Teachers at this school were generally confident about the transition of children into Year One because:

- One of the Reception teachers was also moving to Year One.
- The Reception teacher and the 'other' Year One teacher would be planning together and therefore sharing knowledge about the children.
- They felt reassured because the head teacher had an Early Years background and was keen for the Reception teachers to influence practice in Year One.
- They anticipated an effective use of Foundation Stage Profiles for planning in Year One (they had previously been shelved and unused).

This school was distinctive in that the adults in Reception Class and Year One had Early Years backgrounds. They were confident that they could provide experiences that enabled the children to gradually move towards more formality, but retain ample opportunities for play. The Reception teacher who moved to Year One celebrated the fact that along with the children she too was undergoing transition.

Meadow Lane School

The teachers at this school were happy about the preparation the children had for transition in that there were meetings for parents and opportunities for the children to visit the new classroom. The Key Stage One teachers did not have any influence on the process. There were anxieties expressed by the teacher who was moving from nursery to Year One because she was told that she would have to incorporate play into the formal teaching and she had not done this previously. This advice had come from the local authority. The teacher was unable to articulate her thoughts on how this might be accomplished. She was being told what she must achieve but not how to do it. There appeared to be the added issue of differences in opinion amongst the teachers involved regarding the philosophy and practice that would suit the children moving from Foundation Stage to Year One. There was a training need here to improve the knowledge, confidence and expertise of the Year One teacher to address requirements to provide for play in addition to more formal teaching.

Comparison of the case study schools

Although each school had movement of teaching staff between the two key stages (Foundation Stage and Key Stage One), the impact of this was not always positive and differed between schools. Teachers of High Bank School claimed that this was the most positive aspect of transition at their school. However, the Year One teacher was restricted in her use of the Foundation Stage Profiles for planning and in her provision of suitable experiences because of the pressures from Key Stage One colleagues and the rest of the school. It is interesting that, in contrast, the teachers of Park Green School with similar movement of teachers had more satisfactory experiences, which may be due to the support of a head teacher with Early Years experience. The Meadow Lane School case study illustrates that moving teachers from the Foundation Stage into Key Stage One cannot guarantee a successful change in approach incorporating more play. The teacher was not confident in achieving a balanced provision that incorporated adult-led activities and opportunities for child-initiated activity. These issues will be addressed more fully in later chapters.

Discuss

- What professional development would be suitable for teachers who feel insecure about incorporating play into Year One practice?
- What information should be given by the Reception Class teacher to the Year One teacher to support preparation and planning for the new class?
- What is the impact of line managers?

Key messages

- Factors may vary between different geographical locations.
- Parents want to know about what is expected of their children through transition.
- Careful consideration should be given to the nature and amount of information required from Foundation Stage teachers to inform planning in Year One.
- Year One teachers have to deal with conflicting expectations of them.
- Some Foundation Stage teachers feel confident about their ability to impact on the provision in Year One.
- Knowledge of Foundation Stage practice is considered by Early Years teachers to be advantageous to working in Year One.
- Year One teachers need to have knowledge and expertise to provide suitable experiences for children going through transition into Key Stage One.

4

Preparation or practice?

Chapter content

The chapter will examine some of the issues around transition between Reception Class and Year One and consider the impact of preparation and practice on this process. It begins by looking closely at what happens during preparation for transition, in which two aspects are covered: establishing familiarity, and consideration of practice, using three case study settings as examples.

It then examines the impact of changing practice as part of transition. This compares Reception Class and Year One practice in the same three case study settings, and includes children's perspectives.

It concludes with a summary of the issues identified in the case study settings

What happens during preparation for transition?

There are two key aspects of preparation for transition emerging from interviews with children and adults:

1. Establishing familiarity.
2. Consideration of practice.

I found that there was far greater emphasis on establishing familiarity than there is on considering adaptations in practice during the preparation for transition. Both of these are important for successful transition.

Establishing familiarity

There is a need for the adults and children to become familiar with the new environment into which they will move. To this extent the focus tends to be on familiarising the children with the new venue and the adults on readiness for the physical or geographical transfer. I question whether or not this is transition, and prefer to consider it to be an event that is part of the transition process. Nevertheless, schools do prepare the children for transfer to the new classroom environment in similar ways. This is valuable as children feel sad about what they are leaving behind and anxious about what they may encounter (Fisher, 2009). White and Sharp (2007) found that children's interviews about anticipating Year One indicated they were concerned about the location of the new classroom, how to find it and the layout of the room. Most of the schools they studied held moving up days in which all the children move up to their next classroom and teacher. They also found that some children held misconceptions about the move, such as a child not realising that all his friends were moving with him. These could be discovered and dealt with through visits and discussions with the children.

Discuss
- What steps do you take to enable the children to become familiar with the new environment they will be entering?
- Are parents involved in this process?

Consideration of practice

In the following three case study settings consideration was mostly about the children and adults becoming familiar with each other and with the new environment. This should not be undervalued. It is well known that a sense of security is important to the child and that intellectual development is likely to be more effective if there is strong social, personal and emotional development (Siraj-Blatchford *et al.*, 2003). How the children learned as a group or individually was not given as much attention.

Riverdale School

Preparation for transition from Foundation Stage to Year One followed a similar pattern to previous moves between the phases of the Foundation Stage. The new teachers visited the children in Reception Class to get to know them and for the children to get to know the teachers. The purpose was mostly to get to know one another within surroundings in which the children were familiar. The children also toured the new classrooms. A meeting was held with parents to inform them of the new routines in Year One and to introduce the teachers. Teachers of Reception Class and Year One met to discuss particular issues and needs relating to the children. The kind of information shared in these meetings was about any developmental delays and health issues. The Reception Class teachers prepared additional assessment information to Year One teachers at the request of the manager of Key Stage One. It was evident that the children were confident about who was going to teach them in Year One, where the new classroom was and that they would be with their friends. This may be partly because the new classroom was in the same building and in the adjacent room. Most of the children either showed indifference or were looking forward to moving to Year One. Only two children out of the two classes showed anxiety about leaving adults they enjoyed being with and the 'hard work' of Year One.

At this school the focus for consideration was the developmental stages of the children and familiarity with routines. There was little evidence that there was consideration of practice during the preparations for transition.

Low Vale School

Preparation for transition in this school did not involve meetings between the Year One teachers and children. One reason was that one of the Year One teachers was currently one of the Reception teachers. She was involved with all the children in Reception during free-flow periods in which both Reception Classes shared the same outdoor area. The other reason is that the second Year One teacher was only appointed towards the end of the term and had not been able to visit the children. The children briefly visited the new classrooms at the end of the year. A meeting was held with parents to inform them about routines and also approaches to learning in Year One. A meeting was held between the two 'new' Year One teachers during the summer period to discuss approaches to learning that were to be different from those in the previous Year One. During a discussion meeting, all information regarding the progress of the children in Reception Class was handed to the teacher who was moving to Year One. This meeting was about the personal, social and emotional development of the children as well as progress in learning. There was a noticeable lack of anxiety from the children in this school with regard to transition. Many of the children said that they looked forward to Year One.

During the period of preparation for transition there was significant evidence of consideration of practice. This was probably because the school had reviewed its policy on practice in Key Stage One, intending to introduce a more play-based approach. The less attention given to considering familiarity was probably due to the particular circumstances at that time.

Green Bank School

At this school, procedures for transition preparation had been set by the local authority. The school followed these procedures and did not have any additional ones for this setting. There was a meeting with parents who were also shown around the new classroom and adjacent area. The meeting explained the new routines and that there would be a more formal approach in Year One but still opportunities for play. This philosophy was encouraged by the local authority but did not represent that of the teacher. Assessment records, including the Foundation Stage Profiles, were passed from the Reception teacher to the Year One teacher but there was no meeting; this was due to relations within the setting and not because of the local authority procedures. The children were taken to the new classroom, with the focus being on geographical location in relation to their previous room. As this was nearby it did not seem to have much impact on the children. The children already knew the Year One teacher as she had been their teacher in nursery, but she visited them at the end of Reception Class. The children seemed reassured that it was someone familiar to them; several of them spoke of it positively when interviewed.

At this school there may have appeared to be consideration of practice at meetings with parents, but this was in compliance with the local authority. There was little evidence that practice was fully considered within the school. Instead there was greater focus on familiarity.

Discuss

■ Should the staff at each school consider the change in practice when making preparations for transition to Key Stage One?

The impact of changing practice as part of transition

This section will firstly look at each of the three case study settings listing features of practice in each phase or key stage. In each case this is followed by children's viewpoints on the practice. It will then explore any issues.

Features of practice at Riverdale School

There was a loss of opportunities for children to initiate their own activities in Year One, but fewer interruptions when children were able to purse their own interests. The adult–led activities of Year One were more clearly differentiated than in Reception Class (Foundation Stage). The loss of access to the outdoors for most of the day was noticeable.

TABLE 4.1 Riverdale School

PRACTICE IN RECEPTION CLASS	PRACTICE IN YEAR ONE
• Strong emphasis on play and freedom of movement for majority of the day • Very little adult involvement in play other than formal observations and occasional support requested by children • Periods of play sometimes long and other times brief and abruptly halted for teacher-led input • Designated half hour group teacher-led sessions • Priority given to speaking and listening within the groups, and social skills • Almost continuous access to the outdoors • Ample opportunity for children to make decisions • Able children not challenged in play or teacher-led activities • Snack time always at same time and organised in groups with an adult overseeing children self-serving	• Mornings tend to be formal, teacher-led carpet input followed by activity set by teacher • Teacher-led activities are interactive and use props • Afternoon group work with teacher, and access to role play or workshop when not with teacher • Access to outdoors limited to designated school playtimes and very occasional teacher-led activity • Although free movement and play opportunities are limited, they are seldom abruptly halted • Evidence of whole class tasks in line with school projects showing that there is a strong influence on practice from rest of school • Teacher-led activities clearly differentiated and targeted support for some children

Children's stories at Riverdale School

Child A

I liked being in Reception Class. The teachers were fun and told good stories. Sometimes I could play on my own and sometimes I could play with my friends. I liked to play on the computer and then I would go outside to see what I could do out there. Sometimes I just listened to what other people were doing, or I would look at a book. I wanted to stay in that class.

I did not like being in Year One. I don't like sitting listening to the teacher on the carpet. We have to do things the teacher tells us and sometimes I am not sure why I am doing it. Sometimes the things we do are OK but I would rather choose what to do.

Child B

It was OK in Reception. But I didn't like the star chart. Your name went on there when you did something good for someone else and I never was on there; it wasn't fair! In Reception I used to play with my friends in class and outside. I would tell them stories about what I had been doing at the weekend and we would act them out. My friends listened to me. We didn't like it when we had to stop for snack time, especially when we had only just started! I really enjoyed talking to the teachers. This was in group time; they were a bit too busy to talk when we were playing doing their jobs. But they were nice.

I was glad I moved to Year One because I am grown up and I want to do really hard work. My dad wants me to do hard work. We do lots of hard work in Year One. I had to go and play in the role play corner this morning because Miss was doing some painting with some children; they were making a display. I don't want to play.

Child C

I was happy in Reception Class because we could play nearly all day. Sometimes we had to go to the teachers for a story or to play a game. I liked playing with my friends the best. We could make things in the construction corner. I was good at that and was good at the marble run, but sometimes someone would come and spoil what I had done and I had to start again. I didn't want to talk to the teachers, and just wanted to play.

I was really worried in Year One because it was hard work, I could not do it. My teacher was nice but I couldn't play anymore. Sometimes in the afternoon we were allowed to choose what to play with and I used to go in the workshop room because there were lots of things there and the teacher couldn't see me.

Each child's perspective on the differences in provision between the two phases is personal to them. There is recognition that there is a loss of play and an awareness of 'hard work'. Child B's more positive comments about work possibly reflect expectations from home.

> **Discuss**
> - For each child consider the reasons why he feels differently about experiences in each phase. What adjustments to practice would you recommend to the teachers in each phase?
> - Would this make the transition between the two phases less problematic for the children?

Features of practice at Low Vale School

At this school the teachers considered changes in practice and made adjustments towards the end of Reception Class in preparation for Year One (Key Stage One). There were opportunities to play in both phases, but access to the outdoors became restricted in Year One.

TABLE 4.2 Low Vale School

PRACTICE IN RECEPTION CLASS	PRACTICE IN YEAR ONE
• Well planned teacher-led inputs were interactive, differentiated and short • Play areas were carefully planned to incorporate resources that enabled children to practice what had been taught during teacher-inputs • Children self-registered for chosen activities and this was usually in-between any ability-group activity led by the teacher or assistant • Teachers never engaged with children's play • Access to the outdoors was infrequent and was more likely to be in the afternoons • When the outdoors was available, it was usually for longer periods than indoor free play time • Snack time occurred over an hour when children could register and self-serve • Towards the end of Reception snack time was limited to reflect Year One practice and children took snacks outdoors for playtime	• Well planned teacher-led inputs were interactive, differentiated and short • Play areas were carefully planned to incorporate resources that enabled children to practice what had been taught during teacher-inputs • Activities directed by the teacher, following formal inputs, often made use of the play areas within the classroom • Free choice of play activities was occasional but in addition to independent activity directed by the teacher • Playtime was the same as the rest of the school, and this was the only access to the outdoors

Child A

I liked Reception Class. I could do writing on my own and sometimes I sat with the teacher doing things and writing. I liked this but sometimes I had to do this too many times and I wanted to play. We did interesting things with the teacher and I learned lots of things. I would have liked to play more, and sometimes I had just started playing when I had to go to the teacher to work and I felt cross. It was good when we went outside because I could play with my friends for a long time and I like football. We played with the cars and we took turns; sometimes we fell out but we made friends.

Year One was really good. I liked the work and I liked the teacher. We did interesting things and I could do the work. I did some writing all by myself in the play area, but we did not have very long to play. I was happy in Year One, but it would have been good to play out. I like to play football and like playing with my friends outside; you can't choose what to do inside.

Child B

I liked being in Reception Class. We had some good stories and I really liked doing maths with the teacher. We sometimes played maths games and I was good at that. We had things to play with and I used to try undoing things to find out how they work. I also liked to make things in the construction area but we had to undo it at tidy-up time. I didn't like it when I just started playing and we had to go to the teacher to work. Sometimes we could go outside to play and it was good. I love football and I like playing with my friends outside.

Year One was OK. I could do the work, but I wanted to investigate things and we were too busy working. It would have been good if we could have played out more.

Child C

I liked being in Reception Class. We did good things with the teacher and I didn't have to sit on the carpet for too long. I don't like to sit. When we didn't have to do work we could play. My favourite thing is playing outside; I want to be outside all the time. I used to wait for the teacher to open the door. I am really good at football. Sometimes we talked about things with the teacher and I could tell the class lots of things I knew.

I had a nice teacher in Year One. She talked to me. I listened to her when she was teaching us and we did not have to sit too long. The teacher did interesting things with us. I sometimes got a bit mudded up when we were doing things but the teacher helped me. I really miss going outside; we never go out!

For these children the differences in practice between the two phases were less pronounced than in the other two case study schools. The main feature they missed was access to the outdoors.

Discuss

■ For each child consider the reasons why he feels differently about his experiences in each phase. What adjustments to practice would you recommend to the teachers in each phase?

■ Would this make the transition between the two phases less problematic for the children?

Features of practice at Green Bank School

At this school there was a marked difference in practice in the two phases. Reception Class had a balance between formal and informal practice. In Year One there was much more formal practice with very little opportunities to play other than designated school 'playtime'. The contrast in practice caused difficulties for the children.

TABLE 4.3 Green Bank School

PRACTICE IN RECEPTION CLASS	PRACTICE IN YEAR ONE
• Occasional access to outdoors in addition to school playtime • Games and wide range of resources available for children to access when they are not working with the teacher or assistant • Children able to move freely and choose from resources • Resources sometimes are enhanced to enable children to follow up on adult-led activity • No adult involvement in play unless to deal with issues • Teacher inputs on carpet for short periods • Some differentiation of teacher-led tasks • Teacher-led activities generally interactive • Equal balance between formal and play but no real evidence of links between the two	• Limited access to outdoors • Formal adult-led every morning • Emphasis on whole class adult inputs on carpet followed by directed tasks • Limited resources for play within the classroom • Nearby resources for play seldom made available to the children • Adult inputs tend to last for over 30 minutes • Adults do not get involved in play or plan enhancement of resources to compliment teaching • Adult-directed activity for children invariably involves writing in books or on worksheets • Very limited differentiation

Child A

I liked Reception Class. Our teacher helper was really good. We used to talk to her a lot. I could play with my friends and I liked to play with the sand and water and the construction. I could play counting games with my friends. I was good at that; I used to win!

I couldn't do the work in Year One. It was really hard. Miss told us all about it, but when I had to do it all by myself I got stuck. I was glad my friends went to Year One as well. One day my teacher did a funny game when we were doing sums with her and we all laughed. Sometimes I felt sleepy when we were on the carpet listening to the teacher but she never told me off!

Child B

I learned lots of things in Reception Class. I like to talk to my friends, and sometimes our classroom helper talks to us when we are having our snack. I don't like talking to adults very much but she is a nice lady. I enjoy playing board games and I like counting. My favourite time is when we can go to the play area as we have fun. I like the sand and water and I like construction. I wish I could play there all day.

I was really worried in Year One. I was really good at keeping still and quiet on the carpet. I felt worried about the work the teacher told us to do. I wasn't sure what to do. I needed someone to help me. It would have been good to play with my friends in Year One but we were too busy doing our work.

Child C

When I was in Reception Class I was very good at listening to the teacher and doing my jobs. I could talk to the teacher and all the grown-ups who came to our class. When we were allowed to go into the play area it was fun. I played with all my friends and we talked to each other. I like talking to my friends. I was really good at numbers and counting.

I was very bored in Year One. I was a good boy, I always listened carefully. But I could not talk to my friends. Sometimes I could do my work but sometimes I just didn't get it.

The main causes for concern for each of these children are the lack of opportunities to talk and play in Year One and the insecurity of not understanding how to do their work. There were two reasons for this. Firstly there was inadequate differentiation, and secondly there were few practical activities or authentic experiences through which they could make sense of their learning.

Discuss
- For each child consider the reasons why he feels differently about his experiences in each phase. What adjustments to practice would you recommend to the teachers in each phase?
- Would this make the transition between the two phases less problematic for the children?

Conclusions

The preparation for the period of transition, and the practice during this time, impacted on the children's experiences. Each child's experiences are affected in different ways, even within the same environment. As mentioned in Chapter 2, the children themselves construct their own understanding of the world, bringing prior experiences to the new ones in Year One. It therefore is to be expected that the effects of transition will differ. In addition to this the effects of gender and date of birth should be considered. Teachers should take the differences between the children into consideration when planning before and during the transition period. However, there are patterns of commonality in these case studies that are similar to other studies. There are marked differences in the attention to the way children learn. In the Foundation Stage there is greater attention given to *how* the children learn evidenced by the teachers' comments on the need for play and active learning. In Year One the emphasis shifts to *what* the children are learning and fulfilling curricula requirements. 'The recommended pedagogy was far more teacher-led than child-led' for children moving to Year One (Fisher, 2009: 133). Similarly, as with Fisher's (2009) findings, the change from play-based learning to a formal approach was sometimes very abrupt. Where this happened the children were unhappy and struggled with new concepts. In keeping with other research the children associated 'work' with writing and struggled to sit for long periods either writing or listening (White and Sharp, 2007; Fisher, 2009).

The teachers seemed to be aware of the differences so why did they not address the issues for the sake of the children? In the case studies there was awareness in all three settings that there were changes in practice which affected the children.

- In Riverdale where there was a better balance between adult-led and child-led activity the teachers had knowledge of how young children learn and were supported by a manager who was proactive in pushing a play-based approach into Year One. The adults had said they would develop the use of outdoors in Year One but did not achieve this. The children seemed to be happy at this setting and made good progress with learning and development.
- At Low Vale School the teachers also had good knowledge about how young children learn. However, the practice of Reception teachers and Year One teachers was affected by decisions made by people who were less informed about young children's learning needs. In this case just before and during the transition period the teachers were subject to the expectations of others. This included the completion of written records and also involvement in whole school projects during which the children had to complete activities that were not meaningful to them.
- At Green Bank School it was quite the reverse situation. Those with most influence in terms of management at this setting were encouraging a review of practice in Year One, and had indicated support of a move towards greater access to play as a key part of learning. In this case it was the teacher who admitted a lack of knowledge and understanding about how to achieve a balance between formal and informal approaches to learning and teaching. She felt unable to ensure that the children met all learning objectives if she did not control the learning.

In all three case study schools the use of the outdoors as a place for learning did not just diminish, it stopped. The outdoors became a place to have a break from learning. This is in contrast to the school studied by Fabian (2005), which overcame this difficulty by making outdoor learning part of the curriculum for the whole school. Later chapters will suggest ways in which the issues identified in this chapter may be addressed.

Key messages

- It is important that teachers of Year One understand how young children learn best and that the management system of the school supports a balanced approach which suits the needs of the children.
- Children need to become familiar with the geographical location, nature of the environment and the people they will be with if they are to feel secure about transition to Year One.
- Children regretted the loss of opportunities to play in Year One.
- Most children struggled with formal approaches either because they lost autonomy and/or because it prevented them from learning in a way which suited them best; often this involved the loss of physical activity.
- Children missed opportunities to be outdoors.
- Children needed time to socialise with their friends and to talk.

The features of successful transition between Reception Class and Year One

Chapter content

- The first part of the chapter lists the features of successful transition between Reception Class and Year One. This is intentionally brief as it leaves the reflection to the reader.
- The second part of the chapter has case studies of two boys who transferred from the same Reception Class into different Year One Classes. The case studies provide an opportunity to explore reasons for their differing experiences.
- The chapter concludes with a table for teachers to use to reflect on their provision.

Based on the case studies presented in previous chapters, research by Fisher (2009), White and Sharp (2007), Fabian (2005), Sanders *et al.* (2005) and the Primary National Strategy guidance 'Seamless Transitions – supporting continuity in young children's learning' (2006), this chapter presents a list of features that are generally considered to be linked with successful transition. Each of these should be considered in the light of the particular circumstances and cultural features of a school and individual needs of the children. I deliberately list the features at this stage rather than discuss them, so that the reader can reflect on them in relation to his/her own situation. The list does not reflect any order of importance.

- Children are listened to when they talk about what they are interested in and what they feel about moving to Year One.
- Children are informed about how and when they will move to Year One.
- Parents and children visit the Year One classroom together.
- Year One teacher and Reception teacher discuss Foundation Stage Profiles together.
- Teachers and parents regard transition as a process not a sudden event.

- Year One teacher visits the children in Reception Class.
- Year One teacher observes the children playing in Reception Class.
- Reception teacher and Year One teacher discuss the individual learning styles and dispositions to learning of the children.
- Children are familiar with their new teacher before moving to Year One.
- Children understand what is involved in the process of transition and that they will keep their friendship groups.
- Year One teacher meets with parents before and during transition.
- Year One teacher regards the relationships with parents as a key resource for getting to know the children and the way each of them learns.
- Reception Class teacher makes adjustments to snack availability towards the end of the Reception year so that it is similar to that of Year One.
- In liaison with teachers in Key Stage One, the Reception Class teacher gradually opens access for the children from the Foundation Stage outdoor area to the Year One (and Key Stage One) outdoor area.
- Year One teacher adds resources to the outdoors that promote learning and are accessible to the children towards the end of Reception Class and start of Year One.
- Reception Class children begin to mix outdoors with children from Key Stage One before the end of the Reception year.
- Reception teachers record the children's thoughts about moving to Year One and reflect on them with Year One teacher.
- Year One teachers encourage parents to enter the classroom, especially at the start of the year, and foster a sense of collaboration.
- Year One teachers use the Foundation Stage Profiles to plan experiences for the children, built on what they already know, understand and can do.
- Reception Class and Year One share resources that are familiar to the children.
- Year One children have access to resources that continue to enable them to have some autonomy.
- Year One teachers use alternative ways to record children's learning other than getting them to write about it.
- Children in Year One have resources for play that enable them to practise the skills taught in teacher-led inputs.
- Children in Year One are more active when learning.
- Children in Year One do not spend too much time sat on a carpet.
- Any increase in adult-led activities is small and gradually introduced.
- Teachers in Year One have access to professional development to improve their own knowledge and understanding of how to gain a balance between teacher-led and child-led learning.
- Teachers of Reception Class and Year One have time reflect on their practice and how it impacts on children's experiences and learning.
- Where Year One has more creative approaches to learning the children have better levels of involvement.
- Year One teachers continue the use of observation during child-initiated learning for assessment and are therefore better informed about what the child has learned and how the child learns.

Case study of two boys' experiences of transition at Orwell Mount School

This case study shows that, even within the same school where there are meant to be shared philosophies and policies, the experiences of children during transition between Reception Class (Foundation Stage) and Year One (Key Stage One) can be affected by the knowledge, experience and expertise of individual teachers.

The two boys, Jacob and Steven, were in the same Reception Class and had been in the same nursery class. They moved into different Year One Classes at the same school. Jacob moved to Year One A and Steven to Year One B.

The Reception Class teacher had a degree in Early Childhood Studies. She was supported by management that believed in a play-based approach to learning in Reception Class. The school management also expected close monitoring of each child's progress towards the Early Learning Goals and that appropriate support should be provided by the teacher for each child to achieve these and where appropriate to exceed the goals. The teacher planned the teacher-led inputs carefully, differentiating them according to the members of the group, whether it was whole class or small group. These inputs were interactive, of short duration and children were usually fully engaged during these. The various areas of the classroom where children could play were enhanced in such a way that the children could practise their new knowledge and skills gained while with the teacher. The children did not have extended periods of access to these areas and sometimes were frustrated when they had to stop abruptly. However, they enjoyed being able to choose what to do and the opportunity to talk with their friends. Jacob spent much of his free time in the construction area and Steven liked the water and sand area. Both Jacob and Steven liked to play outdoors whenever they got the opportunity. Both of them played football outdoors and were seen developing skills of negotiation when using wheeled toys and role play resources outdoors. Preparation for the move to Year One involved a meeting with parents and a visit to the new classroom with the new teacher. The Reception teacher also spoke to the children about what to expect. Jacob was very articulate when engaged in conversations and very creative when designing. He enjoyed all aspects of mathematics. He could develop stories and made good progress in writing. He had achieved most of the Early Learning goals by the end of Reception Class. Steven was one of the younger children and had struggled with practical tasks such as dressing himself. However, he showed a strong ability in almost all aspects of the curriculum. His grasp of mathematical concepts was good. He was able to talk about how he investigated things in planned Knowledge and Understanding of the World activities. Steven's grasp of letters and sounds was very good, as was his emerging writing. Steven exceeded the Early learning Goals in most cases.

The plans of the Year One classrooms show that they are similar in terms of space and access to the outdoors, but different in the way space is used.

Both Year One teachers did their planning together and stated a belief in a play-based approach to learning, and that they would be 'pushing Foundation Stage practice into Year One'. At the start of the academic year, both teachers said that they believed in using the outdoors, but did not use the outdoors at all except for school playtimes. However, the experiences for the two boys were different.

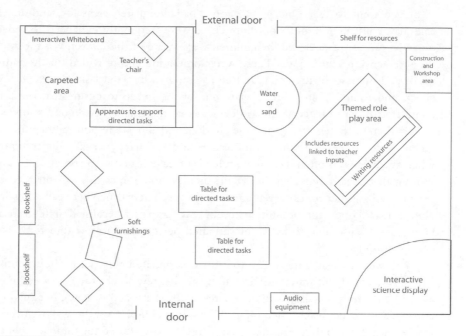

FIGURE 5.1 Classroom A

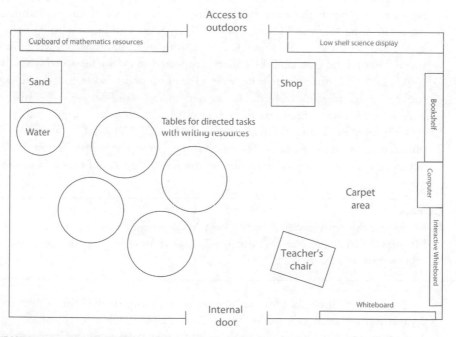

FIGURE 5.2 Classroom B

Steven went to Year One A. The room had designated areas for sand and water, role play, construction and workshop. These were frequently enhanced to reflect the objectives of the teacher and the children were aware of this. Steven was motivated by the interactive teacher inputs. These were stimulating and provided for the individual needs and interests of the children. Before going to directed tasks the teacher would check understanding and also delegate one of the group to ensure that the task was completed as per instructions. It was evident that the teacher used good knowledge of the children to strategically group the children and allocate responsibilities. Steven was a child who cooperated with group leaders and was happy to take the responsibility when asked. He was often seen in the role play area engaged in purposeful good quality writing that usually reflected the taught themes. Sometimes this was directed by the teacher and at other times Steven chose to do this. The balance between adult-led and child-initiated opportunities suited Steven. This was partly because despite his relatively young age he was able to listen for sustained periods and follow directed tasks very conscientiously.

Jacob went to Year One B. The room had designated areas with resources for play. There was a sand and water area, but after the first few weeks there was seldom water available. There was a shop with a few resources (a till and money), but this was not enhanced to reflect teacher-led inputs. There was a display on the wall that related to mathematical vocabulary. An interactive whiteboard was used for some teacher inputs, but the computer was seldom used by the children. Most sessions began with teacher input for the whole class on the carpet, followed by directed tasks within ability groups. These tasks were resourced in the same way as the other Year One Class but often Jacob was unsure of what the expectations were or why he was doing something. In one observation he was seen spending over half an hour looking at photographs that his group had been told to talk about. During that time the photographs were shuffled and moved around the table and the children appeared to be unclear as to what they were looking at or for. At the end of the session the photographs were collected in and Jacob looked completely uninvolved. He seemed to lose confidence in his mathematical ability in this class, which was surprising as I had seen potential previously. I believe that this may be due to the teacher not checking understanding before sending the children to the directed tasks. The teacher did not seem to really know Jacob's prior achievements or interests. There were many fewer displays of enthusiasm during this year.

Discuss

■ Compare the experiences of the two boys. Make recommendations for the teachers in Reception Class and Year One that would make transition more successful for them. Suggest reasons for these.

Based on the list of key features of effective transition at the start of this chapter and lessons learned from case studies in previous chapters, Table 5.1 provides a guide for Reception and Year One teachers to check that they have considered a variety of aspects when planning and reviewing provision during transition from Foundation Stage to Key Stage One.

TABLE 5.1   Transition check for Reception and Year One teachers

ASPECT OF TRANSITION	RECEPTION TEACHER COMMENT	YEAR ONE TEACHER COMMENT
Action taken to find out what the children think about the move to Year One? Before? After?		
Talked to Reception children about what will happen?		
Talked to parents about the move to Year One?		
Sought information about children from parents to ease transition?		
Children have visited the new classroom? With teachers? With parents?		
Reception and Year One teachers have met to discuss the process?		
Reception and Year One teachers have met to discuss the individual needs of the children (including preferred learning methods)?		
Year One teacher has observed the children playing and in adult-initiated activity in Reception Class?		
Year One teacher has explained the approaches to learning to parents and provided opportunities for them to ask questions?		
Reception and Year One teachers agree alteration of practice towards end of Reception and start of Year One? For example, snack time, playtime, access to outdoors, routines.		
Reception and Year One teachers share what they know about the children's views on transition?		
Year One teacher considers how to involve parents and how this may develop during the year? For example, parents access to classroom.		
Foundation Stage Profile information is shared between Reception and Year One teachers?		
Year One teacher uses Foundation Stage Profile information to plan for teacher-led activities?		
Year One teacher uses Foundation Stage Profile to plan the resources and organisation of areas available for children to play?		
Planning in Year One, especially at the start of the year, enables children to be autonomous?		

Continued...

Table 5.1 continued

ASPECT OF TRANSITION	RECEPTION TEACHER COMMENT	YEAR ONE TEACHER COMMENT
Year One teacher develops ways of recording learning other than writing for lessons in science, geography, history and so on?		
Year One teacher considers the use of observations, photographs etc. for assessment instead of written work of children except where relevant?		
Reception and Year One teachers consider sharing resources?		
Year One teacher plans for learning in interactive ways?		

Conclusions

This chapter has shown that we know what are generally considered to be the features of effective transition between Foundation Stage and Key Stage One. It also shows that even within a school where there is a shared philosophy and policy, there can be different experiences for children. The expertise of the teachers is crucial. The transition check enables teachers to check for agreed philosophy, policy and practice. It supports a reflection on the preparation for transition through which knowledge and expertise could be shared.

Key message

■ The knowledge and skills of the teacher are more important than the physical environment when sustaining continuity from Reception Class into Year One.

6

Why should Foundation Stage practice be introduced to Year One?

Chapter content

This chapter attempts to justify the transformation of practice in Year One a) to aid transition and b) because it is more suitable for the way young children learn. It also considers the implications brought about by such a change, in terms of teacher expertise and justification to other adults. In particular it examines the issue of supporting learning and development through play in Year One.

It concludes with a suggested letter to parents to share the philosophy. This is meant to be a starting point and that letters or any other form of communication should meet the needs of the particular school community.

In 1938 Dewey suggested that we need an experiential continuum between the value of an experience in the present time, and the value of the experience in the long term. Either of these is subjective, but is applicable to today's children. Children know what makes them happy and the value of experiences that are fulfilling from the children's perspectives should not be underestimated. It matters to them at the present time. Researchers recommend practice that motivates the children and enables them to reach their potential according to their studies. What is perhaps the most difficult aspect is that as adults we decide what is in the best interest of the children now and in the long term. I argue that political influence makes this not so long term because of the need for evidence within a period of office. Hence the pressure for practice that was deemed to improve the SAT results at the end of Key Stage One.

Children need freedom to move and to choose

Practitioners need to provide opportunities for the child to explore and investigate and make sense of this environment, and have an awareness of their role as part of that environment:

> In terms of human needs, satisfying the need for 'goodness-of-fit' empowers humans to meet the need to instigate a variety of actions, some of which are reinforced. Achieving greater freedom of action allows us to meet the need to discover and exchange new ideas leading to expanded insights.
>
> (Henry, 2004: 303)

It is important that children have freedom to choose and move between experiences as they make sense of their environment and make connections. Each child's construct of this new environment will be unique and it would be inappropriate to make children have identical adult-led experiences for the majority of the time.

Discuss
- Do children have the opportunity to move and choose to meet their own needs?

Children are social beings

Children are social beings and need to learn within a cognitive community in which they share experiences and communicate about them (Radford, 1999). It may be argued that teacher-led sessions are crucial if we are to ensure that children are supported in meeting certain learning objectives. I believe that this would not necessarily be the case if the adults working with the children knew how to make the most of child-initiated activity or play, to support learning. However, 'we seek to impose procedures and conceptualisations in order to meet the requirements of the curriculum and assessments that are in turn imposed upon us' (Radford, 1999: 115). If teachers, like those in Low Vale School, are compelled to fulfil requirements dictated by people in other phases or management, it may be at the expense of quality experiences that suit the children.

Discuss
- What chances do children have to socialise during the school day?
- What are the barriers to this?
- What type of activities would improve the chance to interact socially while learning?

Teachers need to have sound knowledge and understanding

To have the courage to defend the practice one believes is better for the children, teachers need to have sound knowledge and understanding about how children of this age learn. Training for practitioners so that they are able to plan and organise resources and support for progressive learning is crucial (May *et al.*, 2006). It also helps the teacher to articulate to colleagues and parents that the practical and challenging experiences on offer are far more appropriate for young children's learning than formal tasks and over-reliance on writing.

An environment that supports risk taking

An environment that supports risk taking is vital if resilience is to be fostered in the children. Experiences in school could affect the extent to which resilience is encouraged or suppressed. They can develop a repertoire of learning tools that may be applied to different tasks, but their risk taking will vary. Whether or not children will attempt more challenging tasks has little to do with ability and more to do with resilience. Children who play safe feel that success is a crucial indicator of their worth to others. 'Children who have learnt to fear the negative judgement of others tend to internalise the critical voice' (Claxton, 2002). Timid children will become suppressed and will have a fear of risk taking regarding their learning, which may be so well established that it will affect their life-long learning. This crucial need to establish positive attitudes to learning is a really important role for Reception and Year One teachers. Even the more confident child may rein in his adventurous spirit in order to avoid the risk of disapproval if he should fail (Claxton, 1999). A formal approach in which the teacher has a greater control over the agenda and the expected outcomes is more likely to lead to children 'failing' to meet the expectations of the adult. Children instinctively know that the teacher is waiting for the 'right' answer.

Discuss

- How comfortable do children feel if they are asked a question during whole class sessions?
- During small group activities?
- How do teachers encourage children to try new tasks without fear of failing?

Children need to have meaningful experiences

Meaningful experiences are an important aspect of quality provision for young children. It is worth considering the child's learning experiences within the culture of schooling. If there were no institutes of learning such as schools for young children, they would learn through daily experiences in the community within which they live. A natural part of this would possibly include adults passing on their knowledge and skills within the context of the environment in which the child is growing up. Therefore, by placing our children in institutes are we depriving them of real experiences, shared with adults and within meaningful contexts? The preference for learning taking place indoors in many schools does not reflect the variety of experiences that a child may have in the 'real world'. It is crucial that the teacher provide experiences and resources that reflect the world in which the children live, 'then pupil's learning might become much more authentic, flexible and sustained' (Pollard, 2002: 162). Adams *et al.* (2004) found that activities that were meant to promote learning were often 'impoverished'. They assert that if children are offered authentic, stimulating and purposeful experiences from the real world they will be more challenged and satisfied. Sitting on a carpet listening to a teacher is less likely to be meaningful and purposeful than physical activity and engagement that has an evident purpose for the children. Suggestions for such activities are included in the next chapter.

55

> **Discuss**
> ■ How much attention is given to making planned activities meaningful and authentic?
> ■ Are real resources used whenever possible?

The inability to concentrate for sustained periods

The inability to concentrate for sustained periods is often cited as a reason for not keeping children on the carpet for too long. Is this true that children are unable to concentrate for long? My own observations show that, on the contrary, children much younger than those in Year One are able to concentrate for very long periods when they have initiated the activity themselves. According to Lopez *et al.*, (2005) when children are observed in play activities there is a developmental trend in which children gradually become more able to remain on task for increasing periods of time. They found that the study of classroom-structured activities provided information on possible sources of distraction in the context of situations that demand sustained attention. They found that the main source of interruption of sustained attention was social interference rather than other stimuli. Children need social interaction to help them to become involved in a sustained way, as well as opportunities for solitary exploration and thinking time when they choose it. Surely children need ample experience of social interaction in order to achieve the ability to self-regulate, and reach a stage of development when they are able to control their level of involvement in either directed tasks or self-chosen activity?

> **Discuss**
> ■ What kind of activities and resources usually inspire children so that they remain focused on activity for a sustained period?

Opportunities for children to develop social skills

Free movement to choose and play provides opportunities for children to develop social skills. Shin *et al.*, (2004) identified characteristics of emerging leadership behaviour in young pre-school children. One such characteristic is the possession of a 'dynamic and powerful personality' (Shin *et al.*, 2004: 306). They found that the children were creative in their play and in the use of resources. They also found that the young leaders tended to speak out in a group, and use 'assertive, directive and commanding words to exercise dominance' (Shin *et al.*, 2004: 307). The young children appeared to have a global sense of what was going on in the classroom environment and possess a vision of how things should be in the classroom, resulting in organisational behaviour. Similarly, if adults have control over everything the children do, they will not learn how to deal with conflict. This is a vital life skill that will impact on their future lives (Katz, 2004). My own research in Low Vale School showed that the Foundation Stage allowed George to hold an audience with his peers, leading conversations and story developments. He was particularly good at keeping his group of followers on his agenda yet making them feel ownership of the developing story. This often involved problem solving. This showed that at his young age he had the vision and the leadership skills to take others along with him. He also had a strong sense of fairness and would solve conflicts between his classmates by negotiation and reason. Unfortunately during Year One I saw no evidence at all of George practising these skills, because the teacher was more in control of the agenda.

Discuss
- What chances do children have to develop their social skills?
- What strategies are used to promote the development of social skills?

A good balance between teacher-led and child-initiated learning

The organisation of the school day and week to allow for a good balance between teacher-led and child-initiated learning requires a great deal of effort, skills and experience. Having the 'right' amount of teacher-led activity and 'right' amount of opportunities for child-initiated activity is only a small part of the organisation. A primary classroom may be likened to an orchestra, in which the conductor provides individual instrumental tuition to bring mastery to a level commensurate with the rest of the orchestra. The conductor then has to organise, synchronise and communicate so that the whole group can perform together. An Early Years classroom is more like that of an elementary orchestra in which the main body has broken into sections, within which individuals are at various stages of understanding. The task of getting a section to operate in synchrony is difficult, and I suggest that the idea of conducting the whole group with mutual understanding and goals seems to be almost impossible. Taking an approach more like that of the Foundation Stage means 'managing to organise groups of children and individuals so that each child is working to a suitable activity with the right amount of support seems to be the hardest to achieve' (Anderson *et al.*, 2003: 25). It is understandable that teachers and children like to have routine, but routines must be there to support learning, not to prevent it by being inflexible. The way in which time is divided within a day or week is important because:

- Teachers need to ensure that there is an appropriate balance of opportunities for different curricula areas.
- Teachers need to ensure that they have the opportunities to be involved with learning as leaders and (when relevant) as participants in child–initiated activities.
- Children can only remain focused on adult-led sessions, especially if they are sedentary, for short periods.
- Children need long enough periods in which to explore, practise and make connections.

This last bullet point is very important for opportunities to learn and for children's well-being. We should avoid dividing time into slots that are convenient for the adults and the rest of the school, but are detrimental to children's progress. This is not a suggestion that the children should not take part in whole school activities, rather that these should be considered for their worth rather than habit. The amount of time and duration of timed slots given to play is significant. Often children have just become engrossed in an activity, when they are removed to join another activity that is part of the routine of the setting: 'This means that we are not offering children enough time to learn in any depth or to practise and return to learning, the process that enables children to securely embed a concept in the mind' (May *et al.*, 2006: 148).

Discuss

■ What are the barriers preventing a well balanced provision that allows good quality, adult-led learning and good quality child-initiated learning?

The lack of sustained periods for concentration

This 'chunking' of time, particularly in school settings, prevents children from developing their thoughts over a sustained period and consolidating their learning. If the resources are tidied away after each time slot they are unable to return to an activity and make connections. The children need time to become deeply involved in their learning, to think things through and to solve problems. The chunking of time into small slots is not helpful in developing autonomy as 'it militates against children being able to make decisions about how to spend their time' (May *et al.*, 2006: 148). It is also recognised and accepted that children may want to spend hours engrossed in an activity (Nurse, 2001). Adams *et al.* (2004) found that children were often called away from deeply involved play to attend to adult-led activities that were less challenging. The children observed at Riverdale School showed agitation visibly and verbally when they were interrupted during child-initiated activity. This was more profound if they were just getting involved in something after about ten minutes. In these circumstances it is probable that the children were being allowed to play to fill gaps in between teacher inputs rather than for the value of play itself. I argue, therefore, that it is better to have fewer but longer periods of uninterrupted play in which children can move and choose than to have lots of brief periods that have little value and cause dissatisfaction when abruptly halted.

A fluid environment in which children and adults can explore ideas, share thoughts, solve problems, develop accounts, collaboratively reflect and evaluate, needs to have enough flexibility to allow this to happen. Flexibility is not just about the duration of slots of time, but also in both children and adults making adaptations to accommodate developments. Provision for this requires commitment and belief so that sustained shared thinking can contribute to intellectual development. This is through the contributions, development and extensions of thought from all parties, including any adults or children involved (Siraj-Blatchford *et al.*, 2003).

Discuss

■ When planning, to what extent do you focus on a) how targets and learning objectives will be met through your teaching and b) the needs of children to have periods of uninterrupted exploration and investigation?

Play is an important aspect of learning

Play is an important aspect of learning for young children. Play satisfies a need for young children and supports their personal, emotional, social and intellectual development. There are some people in the world of education who appear to believe that play is something children need to do in the early years before they get down to 'real work' when they enter Key Stage One. Not everyone values play as an essential aspect of experiential learning, but rather as a simple opportunity to 'let off steam' so that the children can then concentrate on learning. Moyles (2005) describes some of the many theories on the role of play throughout the twentieth century including metacommunication, transformation, stimulation, learned behaviour, therapy, cognitive adaptation, and psychoanalytical. She suggests that the theories of Piaget (1998), Vygotsky (1992) and Bruner (1980) gave encouragement to those who supported play as a learning behaviour. Piaget believed that children had to act before doing things in their heads (operation), and Vygotsky emphasised the importance of social interaction during activity. Bruner followed Piaget then became influenced by Vygotsky's idea of interaction, adding the notion of 'scaffolding'. It is not difficult to understand these theories, which all seem to have merit, and I would suggest that play is diverse in its nature and purpose, and at any one time is fulfilling any number of roles. For Year One teachers it is crucial that they believe in the role of play in learning if they are to be fully committed to its inclusion in their provision.

Broadhead (2007) advocates open-ended role play with no or fewer themed areas to give children the freedom and autonomy to bring their own experiences to play. However, this may have its limitations because the practitioners will provide the resources and location with which the children construct the play. When examining play in a Year One Class, Broadhead and English (2005) found that the location of the role play influenced the gender ratio of those attracted to it. A role play area near a brick wall outdoors was more likely to attract boys, but if placed indoors near to the 'home area' it attracted more girls. The practitioners in this study learned that the Year One children were more involved in cognitively challenging experiences when the role play was open-ended. It also shows that even when adults are not directly involved in play, they influence it. Creativity in role play is an intellectual activity that 'operates through thought and insight' (Broadhead and English, 2005: 73). The children are able to be resourceful, innovative, problem solve and search for meaning. Broadhead and English (2005) question whether the increase in teacher-driven learning experiences at the end of the twentieth century have reduced the opportunities for children to search for meaning that is personal to them, and perhaps limited their potential to be creative. This is not a suggestion that adult-initiated activity is unimportant for learning, rather that there needs to be a careful balance, so that opportunity for children to direct themselves towards activity in which they can become preoccupied and which fulfils their personal need to seek meaning, is not eroded.

Adult-supported learning and development through play

It is important to consider if and how adults should support learning and development in play. In the *Study of Pedagogical Effectiveness in Early Learning* (SPEEL), Moyles *et al.* (2002) found that adults did not understand their role in children's play and its importance as a vehicle for learning. They observed that practitioners found both intervention in learning through play and the concept of scaffolding challenging. In the case study at Low Vale School two of the teachers admitted that they would like to feel more confident about supporting children in play. One teacher at Riverdale school said she knew that it was considered to be a good thing to be involved in children's play, but regretted that she did not have the time as she was too busy ensuring the children met their learning objectives in her taught sessions. At Green Bank School the Year One teacher was anxious about the expectation of incorporating 'continuous provision' into the classroom. She could not envisage an environment in which the children could have choice and in which she could be sure they had met all the objectives. This is perhaps the main barrier to introducing Foundation Stage approaches to Year One. That is, the teachers need to feel confident that children will meet all the required objectives if there is a greater expectancy to provide opportunities for play.

Discuss

■ How confident are teachers in supporting learning and development through play?
■ How confident are you that you can sensitively support children during play so that they make progress in gaining insight or develop new skills?

Teachers in Year One need time to practise and improve their own understanding of:

■ How play supports learning.
■ How they can support learning through play without interfering.

In order to do this they need to reflect on how they have supported such learning, and a collaborative approach to this within a team would be mutually beneficial. Table 6.1 is a reflective tool for teachers and assistants to complete as soon as possible after involvement with children's play. This was first developed for student teachers who were concerned that their planning files looked thin in comparison to those teaching older children. The reason they gave was that more time was devoted to play for which they had no plans or evaluations. This implied a lack of value given to play. The form was designed to encourage recording of support of play for learning and also to be a tool for reflection on that support. It can be adapted to suit the needs of schools and teachers and can be used for professional development.

Guidelines for completion of 'Supporting learning and development through play'

The following are prompts and it is assumed that other questions and/or suggestions could be added.

Classroom area

Remember to say which area this is, or whether it involves more than one area. Also state if it is outdoors, indoors, or if there is continuity between the two.

TABLE 6.1 Supporting learning and development through play

Classroom area (area of continuous provision)
Context
Date/time/duration
How I supported learning
Evaluation

Context

- Child to child.
- Child and adult.
- Independent activity.
- Was there a particular area of learning involved?
- Are there links to the particular needs of the child?

Date, time and duration

The duration of the activity may last for several minutes, half an hour, or may continue across the day (if it is a sustained project). This will affect the amount you will be able to discuss in the next section.

How I supported learning

- Did you use open-ended questions? Examples?
- Did your questions lead to a next stage of learning?

- Did you make any connections with previous learning/experiences?
- Were connections made between the previous learning and new learning?
- Did you model thinking skills?
- Did you 'think out loud'?
- Did you encourage the child(ren) to articulate thoughts when appropriate (without interrupting trains of thought)?
- Did you enable the child(ren) to be independent, make mistakes, be autonomous?
- Were you able to provide resources (material or human) to improve learning?
- Did you consider whether or not you needed to step back to avoid interference?

Evaluation

- How successful were you in enabling a child's learning to move forwards?
- What do you think the child(ren) may know, understand, or can do that he/she was less able to do before your involvement?
- What made some aspects successful?
- If it were possible to go back and start at the beginning, is there anything you would do differently?
- What might be the next steps for the child(ren)? Resources? Time? Adult support?
- Did anything surprise you?

Discuss
- How can quality learning and development take place through play?
- What is the role of the adult?
- How can you ensure that adults working in Year One develop the necessary skills to support such learning effectively?

Partnership with parents and families

A key feature of the Foundation Stage that should be continued into Year One is the strong partnership with parents and families. For this to happen it is important that the philosophy of those teaching in Year One is shared with the parents. Often parents have opposing views on what should happen in Year One. There are those who believe that Year One is when 'real work' begins and that Reception Class is for playing and preparing them for Year One. Others worry that their child will be unable to cope with a more sedentary style of teaching involving sitting and listening for long periods. This is often gender related as parents of boys are more likely to be concerned about the difficulties of sitting still. Fisher (2009) found that the majority of negative responses from parents regarding transition to Year One came from those with boys, and that both parents and teachers were aware of the difficulties encountered by children with summer birthdays. In the Low Vale School case study it was Elliot who the Reception teachers expressed concerns about because of his late birthday, and he did indeed struggle to cope with formal approaches in Year One.

Discuss

■ Should there be special arrangements for children with summer birthdays, during and following the transition to Year One?

■ In what ways could routines, organisation and resources be adapted to cater for their needs?

■ How might parents be involved in determining the needs of younger children?

It has already been suggested in this chapter that the teacher of Year One needs to have particular skills to develop and manage provision that is balanced between formal and informal, is interactive, engaging, meets individual needs, is challenging and in which there are adequate periods of time in which to accomplish various tasks. In some cases this requires initial training and in all cases requires continual reflection and evaluation. To share this philosophy with parents is perhaps difficult when it is hard to articulate such a complex approach amongst colleagues. The following letter is a simple suggestion that could be customised to suit the culture of any school.

Dear Parents,

We are looking forward to welcoming your child into Year One Class.

It is important for us to know your child well, so that we can support him/her to reach his/her full potential. We have already enjoyed some time with the children and look forward to meeting you. We really value what you, as a parent, can tell us about your child's interests, concerns, newly discovered skills, experiences and so on, that will help us to plan appropriately. It is hoped that you will continue to liaise with us during the year so that we can do our best for your child. It is well known that children have greater success when parents and teachers work in partnership.

In Year One we try to have an engaging curriculum in which children are active, enthusiastic and keen to learn. Our classroom offers opportunities for the children to have choices and play, this helps in their transition from Reception Class. We believe in a balance between formal approaches in which the teacher takes the lead and also play. Our teacher-led activities are carefully planned, well resourced and interactive so that all children are fully engaged and meet the learning objectives. If your child comes home and says he/she has had an enjoyable day it should mean that there has been lots of learning! Sometimes your child will be involved in their own initiated activity (or play) and will probably be unaware that the teacher and assistants are subtly supporting them with their investigations, inventions, language development and problem solving. Our play areas are carefully resourced so that the children can continue the learning that has been introduced by the teacher, as we recognise that repetition is an important part of learning at this age. We also monitor the use of these areas so that the particular needs and interests of individual children are catered for.

It is our wish that your child will make good progress in all aspects of the curriculum this year, and will grow in confidence and enthusiasm.

Yours sincerely

A.N. Other

Key messages

Why should Foundation Stage practice be introduced to Year One?

- Children need freedom to move and to choose.
- Children are social beings and need to learn within a cognitive community.
- Teachers need to have sound knowledge and understanding about how children of this age learn.
- An environment that supports risk taking is vital for self-esteem.
- There should be meaningful and purposeful experiences.
- The inability to concentrate for sustained periods is linked to adult-initiated tasks and is less likely with child-initiated activity.
- Play provides opportunities for children to develop social skills such as conflict resolution and leadership.
- The organisation of the school day and week must allow for a good balance between teacher-led and child-initiated learning.
- Duration of timed slots given to play is significant as children need long enough periods in which to explore, practice and make connections.
- The 'chunking' of time, particularly in school settings, prevents children from developing their thoughts over a sustained period and consolidating their learning.
- Children dislike abrupt interruptions.
- Play is an important aspect of learning for young children.
- Teachers in Year One need time to practise and improve their own understanding of how play supports learning and how they can support learning through play without interfering.

7

A principled approach to planning in Year One

Chapter content

This chapter briefly examines the principles for planning in Year One that:

1. allow children to meet the expectations of national guidelines and
2. allow age-appropriate experiences that will support the development of positive dispositions to learning.

The second part of the chapter considers some examples of planning frameworks for Year One that 1) provide suitable experiences for the children and 2) take into consideration the need to check children's progress against national requirements.

Principles

The development of the 'creative curriculum' in the primary sector should make transition from Foundation Stage into Year One much easier. The reason for this argument is that the features of the creative curriculum being promoted in many schools sit very easily with the principles of the Early Years Foundation Stage guidance. At the very least there is no conflict between the two. 'All our futures: Creativity, culture and education', the National Advisory Committee's report (DfEE, 1999), defined the characteristic features of creativity. The first of these features is that creativity involves thinking or behaving imaginatively. Another feature is that the activity the children are involved in should be purposeful. A purposeful and meaningful activity is more likely to engage children and make sense to them. During meaningful activities it is essential that adults do not dominate the discourse (Ellis, 2005). A third feature of creativity, according to the DfEE report, is that the activities must generate something original. This too requires that adults do not dominate the agenda by controlling the path children take in achieving something (often determined by the adult). It is not difficult for many of us to recall occasions when we have seen adults designing cards for celebrations and controlling the stages a child has to go through in order to complete the task. There might even have been a 'this is one I made earlier' version to reinforce the adult's expectations of the child.

A creative approach needs to be flexible to enable children to have autonomy so that they can initiate their own actions according to their needs and interests. Such an approach provides for initiative when children use the brain to give and gain insights (Henry, 2004). A creative approach enables the cognitive community of children to gain and share experiences, and communicate about them (Radford, 1999). The role of the teacher in such an environment is like that of a coach in which children are supported in transferring their learning to other situations (Fisher, 1995). It is important that the children feel a sense of freedom to be expressive without the fear of having to meet adult expectations.

Creative Partnerships was formed in 2002 to give young people the opportunity to develop their creativity and ambition, focusing on deprived areas. Research into the effectiveness of the partnerships between schools and creative organisations and businesses reveals that there were positive outcomes for the schools and pupils who were involved. Although evidence of the impact on academic achievement is minimal, there are many references to improvements in attitudes and dispositions. Children became more able to work collaboratively, were more confident and willing to take risks, had better communication skills, were more able to improvise and showed more enjoyment in school, possibly accounting for the improved attendance (Ofsted, 2006; Kendall *et al.*, 2008).

Safford and O'Sullivan (2007) found that, according to parents, when children are engaged in creative projects they are more likely to describe these experiences at home. Parents are able to see the positive impact on learning, and on aspirations and dispositions. Parents are also more likely to become involved in creative projects at the school than in the core subjects and inevitably more involved in their children's learning. Funding for Creative Partnerships has ceased under the 2010 coalition government. However, as the government has indicated that it wants schools to have more control over the curriculum there should be no reason for teachers to claim they are constrained and unable to be creative. Creativity is about inspiring children through enjoyable learning experiences. However, I caution against an 'all singing, all dancing' approach that may not carry meaning to the children. It is vital that these experiences are meaningful, purposeful and suitable for the children's particular needs. Authentic experiences are more suitable (Pollard, 2002) as they enable the child to make connections with other experiences and transfer knowledge.

What is important is not just what children learn when they move from the Early Years Foundation Stage to Year One, but *how* they learn. Equally vital is that we consider the impact of practice on the development of children's ability to learn. Open-ended experiences in which children create and seek solutions to problems help them develop thinking and problem-solving strategies (Nutbrown, 1994). Arguably children in the Reception Class will have had opportunities to develop such strategies and had the opportunities to experiment, investigate and make errors without the danger of a sense of failure to meet expectations. The difficult task of the Year One teacher is to continue to foster autonomy whilst feeling confident that they themselves are fulfilling expectations.

Discuss

- Is it true that children in Reception Class have experiences that enable them to develop problem-solving strategies?
- Are there similar experiences in Year One? What are they? Or how could they be provided?

The Year One teacher needs to have a sound understanding of the benefits of a creative approach and the need to improve the children's ability to learn, in order to feel confident that the children in their care will be successful in the short term and the long term. Claxton (2002) identifies four characteristics needed to build learning power in children: resilience, resourcefulness, reflectiveness and reciprocity. To maintain resilience a child should not be afraid to try something new in case he fails to succeed, and the fear of failure is more prominent in adult-initiated activities. A creative approach to teaching and learning allows children to be resourceful, make decisions for themselves, try out new ideas and reflect on these confidently within the learning community of the class. Carr (2002) suggests that the role of a pupil in an early years setting in the twenty-first century will '...become more complex and less well-defined, uncertainty of outcome will increasingly be the norm, and patterns of responsibility for learning will shift towards individual and collaborative forms away from instructions' (Carr, 2002: 99).

This is surely also very important for the learning and development in Year One and beyond. The ability to reflect on changing situations and adapt to new challenges is vital for the rapidly changing world the children are living in.

Discuss

- Share thoughts about the principles that underpin planning. Write a list of the principles you would consider when reviewing planning for a Year One Class. Select the principles that are a priority for you. How would you ensure that these are addressed in future planning?
- How do you foster the development of resilience, resourcefulness, reflectiveness and reciprocity in the children?

Planning

The following planning frameworks are in themes. They are based on projects that have taken place successfully in Year One Classes and are meant to provide ideas for direction when planning. However, they are there as a structure to begin learning and teaching projects and not to control them. Teachers should always feel able to alter the direction of a project or theme in accordance with the developing interests of the children, new ideas brought to the project by the children and changing circumstance or events. Such adaptation to suit developing needs leads to complexity, which requires constant communication, assessment, evaluation and ongoing planning. Therefore the frameworks below are very basic to allow for such adaptation; they are intended to be working documents. It is expected that other planned and unplanned activities, both adult-initiated and child-initiated would develop from these.

67

TABLE 7.1 A blank basic planning frame for use when reviewing planning in Year One

Theme Overarching theme.
Rationale Reasons for doing the topic, what children already know, can do and understand. There may be a special event or occasion that has inspired the topic. Previous experience tells you that this will inspire the children and provide suitable challenges for them etc.
Overall areas of learning to be addressed Perhaps the topic has a mainly creative and artistic focus such as creating music. It may have a spoken and written language focus, or perhaps is leaning towards mathematical concepts and science or technology.
Specific learning objectives to be met Although there will be a wide variety of objectives met by different children in different ways, there will be specific learning objectives that you have identified that must be addressed during the topic/theme.
Location(s) The introduction might be in the role play area and then anticipate that it develops further in the construction area, for example.
Resources List of resources you know from experience and from the children's interests that will be required. Additional resource needs will be identified when observing the children (possibly anticipate some of these?).
General organisation Is there a whole class or group introduction, small group activities, time for play within the theme, series of activities that build on a sequence, planned time for sharing, reviewing, deployment of adults etc.?
Anticipated adult roles Any teacher-led inputs, assistant roles in leading groups or supporting child-led activity, adding resources, observations, records, ongoing planning/responding to developments, offering challenges…
Opportunities for children to investigate, explore, invent, try, practice Group investigations, resources to encourage independent investigation and/or invention, planned time and space for children to repeat and try new things.
Opportunities for differentiation Identify these within teacher-led activities, raised awareness of adults to respond to individuals in terms of support or challenge according to need during teacher-led or child-initiated activities.
Assessment opportunities Identify opportunities to assess children within group tasks through responses to questions, participation, observations, photographs...
Evaluating and reviewing Identify possible stages and/or times for evaluating with the children and evaluating with assistants, possible times for reviewing the progress of the project, reconsider the direction and extensions.

Keeping records of children's activities Plan for keeping records, any writing, drawing, photographic records, collaborative recording of activities using interactive whiteboard or flipcharts, mapping exercises.
Opportunities to share ideas Planned time and space away from adults for discussion, planned time with adults to share ideas, planned slots for adults to discuss observations and how to use these to prompt children to share thoughts.
Links to continuous provision, opportunities for consolidation and connections with prior experiences Plan the organisation of play areas in the classroom and consider the locations and possible links between them (e.g. is it useful for construction to be near shop?), plan resources to be made available to the children to practice what has been introduced during taught sessions, plan time to enhance resources after observations.
Possible follow-up activities Include possible activities to follow on from the original task. This section should be added to as observations of children's developing knowledge, understanding and skills informs possible areas for further development and challenges.
Opportunities to challenge individuals Use of existing knowledge of children to plan more challenging tasks, questions and investigations as appropriate, plan interim review of progress to identify unanticipated opportunities for challenging individuals.
Links to national curriculum guidelines/expectations At the start and once the project is underway review the main learning objectives and opportunities to fulfil national requirements.
Links to Early Years Foundation Stage guidance can be made for the children who did not fully achieve Early Learning Goals

Example theme: baking

This example of a themed project or framework is based on real planning that has been tried and applied in schools. The suggested practical work is indicative of the type of work that can be achieved in Year One that enables the children to make good progress whilst being fully engaged and active. The writing and mathematical work is purposeful and meaningful. It demonstrates that it is possible to have good intellectual development through practical approaches. It also indicates the extent to which many expectations of the Year One national curriculum guidelines can be addressed with an approach that is similar to that of the Early Years Foundation Stage.

TABLE 7.2   Planning frame for baking

Theme Baking
Rationale The children have already done some baking in Reception Class. The oven in Reception Class is available for Year One to use. The topic fits in well with a Key Stage One overall topic of 'celebrations'. The topic provides suitable practical activities that can be shared and encourages collaboration. The topic provides ample opportunities to develop mathematical concepts and language. The topic provides opportunities to use reading and writing for instructions and to use technology.
Overall areas of learning to be addressed • English (reading and writing instructions, retelling stories) • Mathematics (shape, measures, rotation, fractions, sharing, counting, time) • ICT and technology etc. (use of cooker/oven, photographic records, searching for recipes)
Specific learning objectives to be met • To understand that instructions are written in a different style and can include lists. • To understand that instructions follow a particular sequence. • To be able to retell a story in the correct sequence using words and pictures. • To be able to use ICT to represent a story sequence, e.g. slides show or printed photographs. • To understand that a 'bigger' number represents a higher temperature. • To recognise a period of time on a clock/timer as a measure of time. • To begin to recognise units of measurement on a balance scale and understand that larger numbers represent larger amounts. • To count items and begin to share/multiply in rows of three or four. • To use mathematical language to represent shapes. • To be able to talk about half turns and full turns (of cake tins in oven). • To understand that a square or circle can be divided into halves and quarters and that each section is of equal size. To be reviewed and updated after first activities.
Location(s) Whole class introduction in story corner. Use of internet on interactive whiteboard to search for recipes and to record shared ideas. Cooker/technology area of Reception Class for practical tasks of mixing and cooking. Use of designated tabletops for decoration activities. Independent activity within role play, workshop area and book corner.
Resources • Oven, mixing bowls, spoons of different sizes, cake tins of various shapes and sizes, multiple bun tins in rows of three and four, rolling pins of different sizes, cooling trays, storage boxes, cutters of different shapes, baking ingredients (flour etc.), selection of possible decoration materials, shape stencils for 'dusting' etc., weighing scales, recipe books, aprons. • Role play/home corner replicate baking apparatus and recipe books, suitable magazines with recipes. • Library/book corner, recipe books, story books such as Gingerbread Man… • Dough/malleable resources with bowls, rolling and cutting equipment, bun trays etc….

General organisation
- Key adult-led group activity to begin topic of making a birthday celebration cake. Possible ideas of each group making a different shaped cake for comparison. Each group decorate collaboratively (discussion of pattern, colour etc.) mix icing, discuss the change in consistency with added water.
- Second group activity use round cake tins for cake, and discuss how to create a number '6' for birthday cake using the round shapes.
- Develop baking by looking up recipes using books and IT sources. Opportunities for children to create something individually perhaps within a theme such as 'bread' or 'pizza'.
- Within the activities children use digital cameras to record stages in the process. These to be used to retell the story to other groups.
- Teacher will discuss with adults the language and concepts to be explored during each session.
- Appropriate resources added to role play and other areas for children to follow up.

Anticipated adult roles
- Teacher to ensure all adults have the opportunity to consider possible outcomes of the activities, anticipate misconceptions, possible ways to challenge the children.
- Adult to take lead at the start, then gradually let children make choices and negotiate/ collaborate.
- Adults to encourage the children to set oven temperatures and timers and monitor health and safety. Adults to articulate their thoughts and encourage children to do the same. Encourage children to try new ideas.
- Check that children understand new concepts. Adults support children in following instructions but provide space for them to try for themselves.
- Sensitive support in role play and other areas.
- Planned and unplanned assessment.
- Support independent writing and/or scribe.
- Prompt and support individual and group evaluations, encouraging children to articulate how they will make improvements.

Opportunities for children to investigate, explore, invent, try and practise
- Children should be able to create own recipes or their own versions of known recipes and test these.
- Children will be supported in evaluating and making improvements and have the opportunity to try new ideas or improve ideas. Access to various sources for recipes will stimulate ideas that will be shared and discussed.
- Children will be able to experiment with different types of containers for baking. They will be able to try matching different flavours.

Opportunities for differentiation
- During adult-led sessions at the start of the project the adults should consider the verbal communication and use illustrations appropriately depending on the children's abilities. For some children a scribed flow chart using diagrams to represent the sequence of stages in the baking process will support recall.
- The nature of the books is differentiated to suit varying needs.
- The discussions about setting temperatures and timing are differentiated according to the group or individual abilities, e.g. start time and end time, or children work out the actual time taken between start and end time, or given the start time and length of time required work out the end time.

Continued...

Table 7.2 continued

• For temperature some children will be able to be more specific about reading the temperature, while others will just recognise the number getting larger for hotter, or the more you turn the dial the hotter the temperature. For some it will be appropriate to talk about the temperature being put up or turned down. • Measuring weights or capacities can be differentiated according to ability. • Written records can be differentiated, e.g. some children will want to write recipes, others may be able to match instructions to illustrations in a mapping exercise, or to place words and pictures into sequence (using magnetic strips).
Assessment opportunities • General observations of children during activities will tell if they are able to follow or write instructions, measure using apparatus, create new ideas, try them out and so on. Teacher and assistants need heightened awareness of possible opportunities to assess through observations in planned and unplanned activities, to be reinforced by brief planned discussion meetings at intervals. • Focused observations to be used to provide specific information about individuals or small groups to assess ability to read measures, set times and temperatures, calculate amounts of time, use appropriate vocabulary and demonstrate understanding of $\frac{1}{4}$ and $\frac{1}{2}$ fractions and $\frac{1}{2}$ or full turns, share or multiply numbers using bun tins, etc. • Use of photographs to prompt discussion and determine level of understanding. Assessment opportunities to be identified before each planned activity.
Evaluating and reviewing The teacher and assistants encourage the children to evaluate their work at appropriate stages (while waiting for baking in oven, or at the end of the task when food is on a cooling tray, after finishing touches have been added). Adults encourage the children to use the evaluations to inform what they will plan to do next time or if they attempt a new recipe. Questions to support this may include: 'How did you manage to do that?' 'Did you have enough mixture to fill the tin? Why not?' 'I wonder why the edge of this is a little burnt. What might you do next time to make sure it does not happen?' 'Are you pleased with your pizza? What do you think made it so good? Could it be made even better?' etc. Teacher and assistant to evaluate and review the individual activities and review the progress of the overall project. This will inform future planning and support, and will inform any alterations to organisation and supply of resources.
Keeping records of children's activities • Collaborative recordings on flip charts or using the interactive whiteboard (can be printed for permanent records if required). • Annotated photographs. • Mapping exercises. • Written storyboards to relevant levels. • Cut and paste pictures in sequence.
Opportunities to share ideas • Practical activities are to be used as time to have conversations about the activity and other ideas that arise directly or indirectly through the activity. • Time will be made at stages before, during and after activities to share ideas. • During child-initiated activity the teacher and assistant will subtly support children in sharing ideas and exploring these together.

Links to continuous provision, opportunities for consolidation and connections with prior experiences
Items related to the planned topics and those that develop through reflection and review will be placed in home corner, book area, dough table. Published pictures, photographs of activities, storyboards etc. displayed to support recall and prompt thought and discussion. Opportunities to access continuous provision for sustained periods to allow children to explore ideas and make connections will be planned. This will not just be used to occupy the children while others are on adult-led tasks.

Possible follow-up activities
- Children as individuals or in groups make books retelling the story of a baking session. Use photographs, writing or adult scribing according to level of support needed. Use the books to retell the story to others. Display books in role play area.
- Make a recipe book of collected recipes, or newly created recipes.
- Collaborative planning for a picnic, gathering data on preferred options, portray on simple bar chart, make lists of chosen items for menu, share baking tasks, arrange plates etc. with opportunities for counting and arranging into sets etc.

Opportunities to challenge individuals
- Use of measures to challenge children by asking children to estimate time, calculate finishing time, estimate measures by weight or capacity.
- Prompt children, as appropriate, to calculate using fractions and sharing and dividing cakes in bun tins, and, for those ready, the same cakes arranged at random.
- Estimate quantities required for size if baking tins, or for a number of small tins. For example, ask: 'Is it necessary to double the measures if we double the number of baking tins?' 'What are the doubled measures?'
- Prompt children to compare plates or containers of baked items, asking what the difference in number is between the two and relate this to subtraction.
- For those more able to write independently, write instructions for others to follow.
- Talk about seasonal ingredients and make links to food sources. Challenge the children to find out for themselves using newly taught skills of searching for information using ICT and/or books.

Links to national curriculum guidelines/expectations
The following are from national curriculum guidelines for Year One, and can be accommodated within this themed project:
1. Create and describe number patterns.
2. Explore and record patterns related to addition and subtraction, and then patterns of multiples of 2, 5 and 10.
3. Recognise the relationship between halving and doubling.
4. Understand addition and use related vocabulary; recognise that addition can be done in any order; understand subtraction as both 'take away' and 'difference' and use the related vocabulary.
5. Understand multiplication as repeated addition.
6. Understand that halving is the inverse of doubling and find one half and one quarter of shapes and small numbers of objects.
7. Use vocabulary associated with multiplication and division.
8. Observe, handle and describe common 2D and 3D shapes.
9. Understand angle as a measure of turn using whole turns, half turns and quarter turns.
10. Estimate, measure and weigh objects.
11. Choose and use simple measuring instruments, reading and interpreting numbers and scales to the nearest labelled division.

Continued...

Table 7.2 continued

1. Listen to each other and adults giving detailed explanations.
2. Use the organisational features of non-fiction texts, including captions, illustrations, contents, index and chapters, to find information.
3. Understand that texts about the same topic may contain different information or present similar information in different ways.
4. Teach pupils to sequence events and recount them in appropriate detail.
5. Use a clear structure to organise their writing.
6. Use the texts they read as models for their own writing.
7. Teach pupils the value of writing for remembering and developing ideas.
8. Include instructions in the range of forms of writing.
9. Gather information from a variety of sources (e.g. people, books, databases, CD-ROMs, videos and television).
10. Present their completed work effectively (e.g. for public display), exploring a variety of ICT tools.
11. Explore and describe the way some everyday materials (e.g. water, chocolate, bread, clay) change when they are heated or cooled.
12. Learn about how to use everyday appliances that use electricity.
13. Recognise that there are hazards in living things, materials and physical processes, and assess risks and take action to reduce risks to themselves and others.

Links to Early Years Foundation Stage guidance can be made for the children who did not fully achieve Early Learning Goals
1. Use language for an increasing range of purposes.
2. Know that information can be retrieved from books and computers.
3. Ask questions about why things happen and how things work.
4. Use simple tools to effect changes to the materials.
5. Manipulate materials to achieve a planned effect.
6. Talk about personal intentions, describing what they were trying to do.
7. Work as part of a group or class, taking turns and sharing fairly.
8. Appreciate the need for hygiene.
9. Select the correct numeral to represent 1 to 5, then 1 to 9 objects.
10. Use ordinal numbers in different contexts.
11. In practical activities and discussion, begin to use the vocabulary involved in adding and subtracting.
12. Use language such as 'greater', 'smaller', 'heavier' or 'lighter' to compare quantities.
13. Show curiosity about and observe shapes by talking about how they are the same or different.
14. Talk about, recognise and recreate simple patterns.
15. Begin to use mathematical names for 'solid' 3D shapes and 'flat' 2D shapes, and mathematical terms to describe shapes.
16. Use everyday language related to time, order and sequence familiar events, and measure short periods of time with a non-standard unit, for example, with a sand timer.

Discuss

- Choose a mathematical concept that you could teach through a baking activity. Discuss how you would plan and assess this. Select a learning objective for language and literacy that is usually addressed in Year One and consider how this could be taught through a baking activity.
- Would the children grasp the concept and remember their learning more or less effectively through this activity or previously used methods?
- What resources and support would you need to bake with the children? How would you justify doing this, in terms of the opportunities for learning?

Example theme: story through art and music

This planning framework demonstrates that the requirements of the Early Years Foundation Stage and the National Curriculum for Year One can be addressed with an interactive approach to art and music. It shows that children who have yet to meet the Early Learning Goals are able to work alongside those who have exceeded them. Readers can add the specific learning objectives for language and literacy related to the story element if required. These have been omitted from this example to allow a focus on linking music and art across the two phases of education.

TABLE 7.3   Planning framework for story through art and music

Theme   Story through art and music.
Rationale   Children need opportunities to express themselves in different ways.   Engaging with art and music is necessary for children to develop skills.   Teachers have a responsibility to discover innate ability that may otherwise remain hidden.   Freedom to express individually and collaboratively through art and music has a positive impact on children's well-being.
Overall areas of learning to be addressed   The main areas of focus are creativity in art and music, with a general link to creating, telling and retelling stories.
Specific learning objectives to be met   • To be able to represent observations, ideas and feelings through art work and music.   • To be able to select resources from within the workshop area and natural environment to represent their ideas.   • To be able to evaluate their own and other's work.   • To be able to talk about how they can make improvements (individually and collaboratively).   • To use experiences, stories and the local environment to work on projects (individually and collaboratively).   • To create 2D and 3D works of art relating to experiences and stories.   • To create sound that represents stories and emotions.

Continued...

Table 7.3 continued

• To use a variety of instruments including own made or natural materials, to create different sounds. • To recognise and discuss different types of recorded music that can be used for different purposes. • To be able to recall and repeat melodies with instruments including voices. • To recognise pattern in music and relate this to pattern in story. • To be able to discuss rhythm, pitch, volume and length of music, particularly in relation to its role in telling a story. • To respond to music with music and dance. • To create music and sounds to use for movement and dance.
Location(s) Suitable space indoors or outdoors to explore manufactured instruments. Outdoors and indoors for exploration of existing sounds and those to be created in the natural environment. For this theme it is anticipated that the outdoor environment might provide greater stimulus for developing a story and for reflecting on the use of art and music to represent the experiences and feelings related to the story. A workshop area will provide resources and space for experimentation with materials.
Resources Assuming the story is to be developed outdoors, the outdoor environment is a key resource. • Photographs of outdoor environments. • Wide variety of painting materials. • Fabric, cardboard, and access to wide range of workshop materials. • Whiteboard and/or flip chart. • Manufactured musical instruments and selection of improvised instruments. • Wide selection of recorded music both classical and modern. • CD player/iPod with speakers, as appropriate for children to use. • Recording devices to record music and story. • Digital camera and camcorder.
General organisation There are five phases to this project. The first three of these can be introduced in any order. 1. Explore sounds and music in groups by listening to recorded music, listening to sounds in the outdoor environment and creating sounds through improvisation. This should get the children used to talking about what they hear, what they like, what it reminds them of, how it makes them feel and so on. It is also an opportunity to begin to talk about dynamics such as rhythm, pitch and volume. They can use movement to express their response to the music. This phase should provide for the children to explore individually as well as sharing thoughts. 2. Explore paintings and photographs of the outdoors. Use contrasting scenes such as a quiet country view and a busy marketplace, discussing the story of each place as the children see it. Compare different perspectives of the children in response to the pictures. Talk about the use of colours and materials. Study a model or statue of an outdoor scene or people and discuss the composition of this and the story it may be telling. 3. Tell a story outdoors using the outdoor environment, including any sounds, as the illustration of the story.

4. After exploring some new concepts in the above phases, in groups supported by an adult, children should collaboratively create a story using the outdoors. This can be done in many different ways depending on the interests and abilities of the children and on the nature of the outdoors you have access to. For example, a group might begin by sitting beneath a tree and talking about who or what might visit the tree by day or night and then the children develop the story from this starting point. Another example might be to go for a short walk with a camera recording the walk and using the pictures to retell and develop their story using the photographs to order the story. Another starting point might be a 'lost' item found in the undergrowth and speculations as to who it belongs to and how it got there. The groups would decide how to record their experiences and how to retell the story for others, expressing emotions and ideas using any combination of painting, modelling, music and sounds.
5. The final phase is for children to be free to create stories using music, art and movement, either individually or with a friend.

Anticipated adult roles
*   During the first three phases the teacher and assistants will have to teach some skills and introduce some vocabulary that will help the children to express their ideas and feelings. A careful balance will have to be met between ensuring the children are introduced to the relevant concepts and giving them opportunity and encouragement to explore and investigate.
*   In phase four the adult's role becomes more supportive and less directive. This requires very skilful adults who can support and gently prompt thought without controlling the direction of the story and its expression. Ideally, the adult should be invited by the children to be part of the creativity.
*   In phase five the adult should have a heightened awareness of the children's activities within continuous provision to look out a) for connections being made between the introductory activities and the children's play and b) for opportunities to support the children's collaborative or individual attempts to express ideas, feelings and stories through various media.
*   In all phases the adult should encourage the children to talk about what they are doing and why they are doing it. This should be done sensitively so that thought processes are not interrupted. In all phases the adult should sensitively get the children to evaluate their work and discuss how they can make improvements and further develop their work/stories.

Opportunities for children to investigate, explore, invent, try and practise
*   Within the first three (introductory) phases the children will have some freedom and encouragement to experiment with ideas and resources. This is to be planned into the activities that are to be initiated by the teacher and/or assistants.
*   Following phase four, the children should have access to space and resources to continue to explore, experiment and invent stories and resources. For this to happen there will be periods of time that are of adequate duration for the children to have deep involvement and try and test ideas. The adults will trust the children to use resources such as workshop materials, musical instruments and recording devices with minimal supervision.

Opportunities for differentiation
The teacher and assistant will observe the children and share information they have about hidden potential in the children. For example, they will note and share observations about the ability to:

Continued...

Table 7.3 continued

1. discuss and consider the use of colour and/or shape to convey meaning or a story
2. share thoughts about the stories that may be portrayed in pictures
3. respond to music in an individual way
4. recognise dynamics in music such as pitch, rhythm and volume
5. talk about artwork (own and/or others) in relation to how it makes them feel and what they like/dislike
6. talk about the use of music to express feelings and emotions
7. use instruments in art and music to express themselves
8. re-present what they have seen or heard
9. recall and repeat melodies with correct pitch and rhythm.

Such observations will be used to challenge children and to provide time and space for individuals or groups to achieve their potential. For example, children with good recall of phrases in music will be given opportunities to use tuned instruments such as a keyboard to compose simple tunes and develop patterns. Children who show an interest in trying different media in their artwork will be provided with a range of resources which enable them to further develop their ideas. Children, who show an interest and skill in evaluating artwork or pieces of music, will be given opportunities to engage with groups of other children and adults who will challenge their thinking by sharing their interpretations and evaluations. Children whose ability to retell stories is improved with the use of photographs will be encouraged to talk about how the photographs can be used to tell a story and explore different ways to do this with support.

The sharing of observations is ongoing but will be done formally at the end of each day to ensure planning is amended accordingly.

Assessment opportunities
Ongoing observations will be the most important form of assessment in this theme so that developing creativity will not be stifled. The sharing of the observations is important because the direction in which the stories, artwork and music develop will always be subject to the developing ideas of the children.

When particular interests, talents and skills have been identified, targeted observations will be used to assess their development for individuals. When appropriate this will be recorded for the purpose of further assessment and children's records. For example, if a child shows a strong ability to accurately recall and repeat phrases in music, an audio recording may be used. Subsequent development that may be in repeating patterns using known phrases will be audio recorded so that comparisons can be made and evidence of progress can be shared with the child and others. An example previously observed is of a child using music to tell an individual story. She used a slow tempo to show someone waking up and cleaning their teeth. She used an upbeat tempo to show the same person rushing as they were late for school and went back to the same slow tempo to show the child arriving at school and sitting down to listen to a story. It was a known tune that was hummed. The assessment led to further development using percussion instruments for a similar purpose.

Evaluating and reviewing
The teacher and assistants will review developments on a daily basis. Evaluating is a key component of this project and children will be introduced to the concept of evaluation in the first phases when discussing art and music collaboratively.

When groups or individuals develop their own stories expressed through art and story adults will support them in evaluating their work and using this to plan for improvements.

Keeping records of children's activities • Series of photograph slides completed by children, with added notes by the teacher and/or assistant will be retained for records. • Annotated photographs will be used to capture developing skills, confidence, processes and achievements. • Observations that are likely to impact on planning will be recorded in writing for sharing and retaining as appropriate.
Opportunities to share ideas Sharing thoughts and ideas will be a constant feature of this project, in adult-led sessions and child-initiated work. However, time and space will be provided for uninterrupted periods so that children can wallow in thoughts, make their own connections and use trial and error.
Links to continuous provision, opportunities for consolidation and connections with prior experiences It is anticipated that the children will engage in group organised activity at the start of the project. Opportunities to explore, investigate and invent will increase following the initial inputs. This is reflected in the increased frequency and increased duration of time slots given for free choice as the project advances. Adult involvement will become increasingly 'light touch'. This will be reviewed twice weekly.
Possible follow-up activities • If appropriate, a small drama production may be planned that uses the story lines and expressions of these in art and music. • A book (or books) could be made telling the stories through pictures/photographs, with either children writing or adults scribing depending on requirements. • A display area or 'art gallery' could be developed with labels that tell the story. Invitations could be sent to families to visit the gallery.
Opportunities to challenge individuals The teacher and assistant will identify individuals showing particular abilities each day, and discuss how to challenge them with resources and support. This will occur during developing activities.
Links to national curriculum guidelines/expectations Key Stage One: 1. Be able to represent observations, ideas and feelings through art work and music. 2. Design and make images and artefacts using a variety of resources to choose from. 3. Review what they and others have done and say what they think and feel about it. 4. Use their experiences, stories, natural and made objects and the local environment to work on projects (individually and collaboratively). 5. Create 2D and 3D works of art relating to experiences and stories. 6. Rehearse and perform with others (e.g. starting and finishing together, keeping to a steady pulse). 7. Play tuned and untuned instruments. 8. Create musical patterns. 9. Listen with concentration and internalise and recall sounds with increasing aural memory. 10. Explore, choose and organise sounds and musical ideas. 11. Know how the combined musical elements of pitch, duration, dynamics, tempo, timbre, texture and silence can be organised and used expressively to create structures such as beginning, middle and end.

Continued...

Table 7.3 continued

12. Know how sounds can be made in different ways (e.g. vocalising, clapping, by musical instruments, in the environment). 13. Know how music can be used for particular purposes, such as a lullaby.

Links to Early Years Foundation Stage guidance can be made for the children who did not fully achieve Early Learning Goals 1. Express and communicate their ideas, thoughts and feelings by using a widening range of materials, suitable tools, imagination and role play, movement, designing and making, and a variety of songs and musical instruments. 2. Respond in a variety of ways to what they see, hear, smell, touch and feel. 3. Choose particular colours to use for a purpose. 4. Work creatively on a large or small scale. 5. Create constructions, collages, painting and drawings. 6. Explore colour, texture, shape, form and space in two or three dimensions. 7. Begin to move rhythmically. 8. Begin to build a repertoire of songs and dances. 9. Explore the different sounds of instruments. 10. Recognise and explore how sounds can be changed, sing simple songs from memory, recognise repeated sounds and sound patterns and match movements to music. 11. Use their imagination in art and design, music, dance, imagination and role play, and stories.

Discuss ■ How would you begin to plan an activity for developing storytelling and writing with children? How might you incorporate art or music into the activity? ■ For all children, but especially those for whom writing is a difficult and laborious task, how would you encourage the children to record their developing story? ■ How would you encourage the children to tell their developing story to an audience? What benefits might this have for story planning and creativity?

Conclusion

This chapter has provided some ideas for planning in Year One that would provide meaningful and purposeful experiences for children, and fulfil requirements. It is an illustration of what is possible and should serve as a stimulus for a creative approach to planning for this phase, as well as enabling a smooth transition in practice from the previous key stage. Such experiences would also be more enjoyable and rewarding for the teachers.

Key messages

■ It is possible and desirable to have a creative approach to learning and teaching in Year One.

■ A creative approach enables children to be autonomous learners, take risks, work collaboratively, and be more resourceful and more reflective.

■ It is possible to have a creative approach and to meet curriculum expectations with good levels of attainment.

Moving to Year One
Opportunity for continuity and for change

Chapter content

This chapter takes an optimistic look at transition through opportunities for reflection, development and children's rights and ideas for change. The section on ideas for change focuses on the four aspects that are common issues during the transition period: outdoors, music, time management and play.

   The topic of play concludes this chapter because it is the most prominent aspect of change from Reception Class to Year One provision identified by teachers. It therefore seems fitting that it should be revisited in the final section of the book before the concluding summary and recommendations chapter.

The transition between Reception Class and Year One represents a boundary between two phases, each with their own guidelines and expectations. Those responsible for each of these phases should rightly concern themselves with the transition across the boundary. This book generally suggests that if Foundation Stage principles move across into the Year One curriculum it will provide familiarity, continuity and improve the quality of experiences for the children. However, this would be simplistic; the transition is also an opportunity for reflection and change.

Opportunities for reflection, development and children's rights

Those working with children are expected to be reflective practitioners. It is important to explore the meaning of the term 'reflection', before studying the different types of reflection, or even different levels. Reflection is related to learning and the representation of that learning, and enables us to consider something in more detail before we re-present it orally or in written form (Moon, 1999). Reflection implies more than simple recollection, it is about thinking through complex ideas. Critical reflection in learning is transformative learning. Critical reflection helps us to review our assumptions so that our thoughts of other's perspectives become more 'inclusive, discriminative and permeable' (Mezirow *et al.*, 1990: 14), therefore improving understanding. It should be part of the preparation for transition.

Teachers from both phases, and others who have responsibilities for curriculum development within the school, need time and space to critically reflect on practice and plan for improvements. Time is precious but this process could form a crucial part of professional development if it is valued by those concerned. I recommend that teachers keep a journal for a short period leading up to reflective meetings. Unlike talking, writing thoughts in journals is private and can incorporate opinions and prejudices. Bolton (2010) argues that writing abstracts offers less access to meaning, whereas writing narratives can help us to deal with everyday issues, feelings, actions and thoughts. The freedom to write expressively will help the teacher to be reflective. The writing may be used to inform discussions during transition meetings about philosophy and practice, reflecting on:

- the impact of various aspects of practice on individual children and collectively on groups of children
- the impact of various aspects of practice on the teacher
- the knowledge, understanding and justification for particular strategies, either used or suggested
- apprehension about expectations
- perceived risks when making change.

It is the sharing of reflections, seeing others' perspectives and giving consideration to others' points of view that can lead to greater insight. Having to articulate one's own thoughts and recordings to someone else almost forces the individual to apply serious thought to what they think and believe. Provided there are protocols for these meetings, conflicting opinions and beliefs that present challenge can enrich and deepen knowledge and understanding. Uncomfortable processes are sometimes necessary to bring about change, but are indicative of the due consideration that has been given, and will result in stronger convictions.

Strong staff development is a common feature of effective settings, as is a positive engagement with parents that is not just an expectation of parental support (Siraj-Blatchford *et al.*, 2003). Knowledge of alternative curriculum models and different approaches to learning and teaching is perhaps an indication that the teachers are reflective practitioners who are open-minded and responsible. 'Reflective teaching is based on teacher judgment, informed by evidence-based enquiry and insights from other research' (Pollard, 2002: 13). Judgements about the quality of provision are value laden, but will be driven by the lead practitioner, who needs to be clear about what is to be achieved and how it should be done. 'Both the training of the practitioner and their individual personality have huge ramifications for the quality of the practice in settings' (May *et al.*, 2006: 144).

If adults have significant impact on the experiences of children, surely they should be reflecting on their own practice and its impact on children's experiences. Moyles *et al.* (2002) found that, in the SPEEL project, practitioners were less able to talk about their own practice than the behaviour of children, and were unaware of their own impact. They suggest that the inability to articulate will have a detrimental effect on pedagogical practice.

Eyles (2007) also found that mentor teachers and practitioners needed to reflect and discuss their practice openly if they were to develop. There are good reasons here for action research as a preferred method of professional development as it would involve practitioners relecting on and discussing the impact of their practice. Table 8.1 provides a guide for a reflective meeting between teachers of Reception Class and Year One, and each teacher should consider each aspect before the meeting. It is not meant to be fully comprehensive, but is provided as a suggested framework for reflection that can be further developed.

Discuss

- What opportunities are there to reflect on your practice? To share ideas?
- Do you record thoughts for consideration and sharing with colleagues?
- What barriers might there be to engaging in planned meetings to reflect and evaluate?
- Would a chance to meet, reflect and discuss be welcomed?

TABLE 8.1   Guidelines for reflective meeting involving Year One and Reception Class teachers preparing for transition

What strategies do I use to support children in creating/telling/writing stories (use of photographs, props, role play, discussion, writing frames, collaborative creation of stories…)?	
Do I seek opportunities to model different ways of writing for different purposes?	
How do I, or could I, teach mathematical concepts through meaningful activity (baking, constructing, weaving, selling, sharing picnics, tally charts for games…)?	
How much authenticity is there in my planned activities (growing plants, harvesting and cooking vegetables)?	
Do I provide the children with real objects and materials to investigate and use (clocks and other apparatus to dismantle and investigate, or tools to use for cooking, gardening and building)?	
How can I bring the real world into the classroom (visits and visitors, parcels/letters/postcards from other places, internet)?	
Do children have the opportunity to explore, investigate and experience natural phenomena (natural woodland, different types of weather)? How could I take advantage of a windy day to investigate its power to move objects or to dry wet surfaces or wet clothes…?	

Have I the confidence to alter plans and take advantage of unexpected opportunities?	
Do I give the children enough time to become immersed in their investigations?	
Do I give the children enough time to develop their play or their stories either through role play or in writing?	
How do I let children know that I value them as individuals?	
How do I show appreciation for the children's ideas and creativity? Is it tokenistic or real? How would a child know?	
Do I make sure I have time to work alongside children, learning with them using sustained shared thinking? How? When?	
Do I listen to children? Do they know I am really listening? How? Do I respond to their interests and needs in the provision?	
Do the children and I make decisions together? Examples?	
Do I challenge children? How? Who? When? Is it in planned activities or child-initiated activity?	
Do I reflect on what I do? Do I discuss this with anyone else?	
Am I able to justify to others that opportunities for play are an important aspect of learning?	
If challenged would I be able to defend my own philosophy for learning and teaching in my phase?	

Table 8.2 is for joint completion when teachers have shared their reflections on provision and are ready to consider continuity and progression during the transition period.

As part of the reflective process teachers consider a) the inevitable changes for the children and b) possible changes in their own practice to accommodate the needs of the children.

It would therefore be appropriate to consider the rights of the child in these changes. Article 12.1 of the United Nations Convention on the Rights of the Child (UNCRC) is about children's participation in decision making. It was ratified by the UK government in 1991. The implications are that a) a child should have a right to express a view and b) the views of the child should be given due weight.

TABLE 8.2 Sharing preparation for transition

Should we ensure that the children are moving towards the type of practice typical of Year One, when they are in the latter stages of Reception Year? Any modifications to routines? Any changes to snack time or lunchtime to make it closer to that of Key Stage One? Timescale? Any increased involvement in whole school activities or events? Do I need to become more familiar with the routines of Year One? Have I discussed transition with parents? With the children?
Should we ensure that practice in Year One is closer to that of the Foundation Stage at the start of the new school year? Could the classroom be organised in such a way as to resemble the Foundation Stage? Should there be opportunities for play that reflect that of Reception Class more closely? For how long? Am I confident in supporting learning and development through play? Any continuing professional development (CPD) needs? Have I discussed transition with parents? With the children?
Have we considered the rights of the child? Before, during and after the process of transition?

It is questionable to what extent children participate in decision making. Even on the lower levels of Shier's (2001) 'Pathways to Participation', in which there is a readiness to support children in expressing their views, there will be varying levels of evidence in some schools. A move to more formal adult-led approaches must make this more difficult to fulfil. Yet, according to Shier, we should be much higher up his pathway if we endorse the UNCRC. This would require a readiness to take children's views into account, have a decision making process that enabled one to take the child's views into account, and a policy requirement that views of the children must be given due weight in decision making.

The 'child's voice' has become a common term often used in relation to concerns that children are not being listened to. Children telling their views, and adults listening to these, are complex. Children might tell how they feel verbally, by their behaviour and what they do not say. Listening to the 'voice of the child' requires skill, commitment and responsibility. Strategies may include noticing, observing, hearing and actively seeking children's perspectives. There are inevitable ethical issues about the adult's role in interpreting the children's views. True listening should involve responding, otherwise it would be tokenistic.

Processes involved in reviewing policy and procedures use adult ways of communication. MacNaughton *et al.* (2003) used a combination of methods to work with processes preferred by the children to express their views. Pictures, photographs taken by children, drawings and actions can be used by children to communicate their views in addition to their verbal expressions. It could be argued that such processes carry more meaning and a greater indication of significance to the child than the spoken word in isolation. The focus on rights is an opportunity to energise the reflective process during the Reception to Year

One transition period as it enables a rethink of the way relationships are created. This can be achieved through the way policies are created and a review of how workers conduct interactions with children.

Discuss
- Do teachers know about the rights of the child?
- Do I consider the rights of the child when planning?
- Have I or my colleagues discussed the rights of the child when reviewing planning? How and when could this be addressed?
- Who should take part in a review of provision that considers the rights of the child?
- How can this be achieved?

Key message

- Transition between two phases each with different guidelines is an opportunity to reflect on practice and rights.

Ideas for change

There are many aspects of practice that can be considered for change. However, there are a few that are particularly pertinent to the move from Reception Class to Year One. The following will be discussed in this section:

- outdoors
- music
- time management
- play.

Outdoors

I discovered that there was a complete contrast in provision for access to the outdoors between Reception Class and Year One in most schools I visited. Although the time allocated to the outdoors and the nature of this provision varied between schools, all the Reception Classes had access to the outdoors during the school day, and it was used for learning and development in addition to recreation. In contrast, in the Year One Classes there was very limited evidence of access to the outdoors other than for recreation in the form of school breaks and physical education. As mentioned in a previous chapter, one of the children reminded me of the basic human right to have access to the outdoors for its own sake. Having observed his strong desire to be outdoors, I asked him why he liked to go out. It was simply because there was no roof and he could see the sky. Understandably, parents worry about their child's friendships and we perhaps overlook their need for solitude to ponder, explore or simply be alone. 'The outdoor area is able to provide solitude and tranquillity because of its space, location (surrounded by gardens and a playing field) and openness to sky' (Harding, 2005: 147).

Meeting learning objectives outdoors

Teachers in the UK may feel the need to provide learning objectives and detailed planning in order to justify continuous access to the outdoors. A study of Foundation Stage classes in Welsh schools, by Maynard and Waters (2007), found that adults tried to keep children focused, and instructed them as they might do indoors. However, there are some aspects of learning that are easier and much more likely to happen and be successful outdoors. Examples of these include digging, planting of seasonal plants, large-scale construction and water play, climbing and mini-beast searches (May *et al.*, 2006). We should not undervalue the additional benefits of improving children's well-being, both emotionally and physically, through continuous access to the outdoors. As already mentioned in Chapter 2 the outdoor space is often larger than indoor space, offering opportunities that cannot be provided indoors.

Risk taking outdoors

The outdoor environment, and especially one that is natural such as a forest school, provides greater opportunities for risk taking; this is especially so for physical activity. The outdoors is an environment in which children sense greater freedom to roam and to be free from reprimands. Carruthers (2007) reports a lack of a sense of adventure in Early Years outdoor provision. She found that children in her study preferred play space outdoors for 95 per cent of the time, and as a result the setting appointed an 'outside coordinator'. She found that boys favoured superhero play and needed to be more active, therefore the outdoors suited their needs more than the more sedentary nature of indoor activities. Jarvis (2007) also found that boys' play tended to be of a high energy level compared with that of girls; this was particularly so when there was 'boys only' play. There was much less 'girls only' play. She found that there was more physical confrontation in boys play, and less vocalisation than for girls. Like Carruthers, Jarvis noticed that the boys liked superhero play, with the toughest of television characters being the most popular. Girls, however, would invite a boy to play and be a monster to chase them. These opportunities to negotiate roles, invent stories and fulfil a need for energetic play and to take risks can be well provided in the outdoors. Smith (2005) defines exercise play as gross locomotor movement that is vigorously active. It may be argued that children need to exercise their muscularskeletal system during this period of development, and this may offer a reason why children are more likely to engage in energetic play when they have been confined to a classroom. Anecdotal evidence would suggest that this is particularly so if the children have been involved in sedentary tasks. Again through anecdotal evidence, I suggest that the number of accidents such as 'bumps and bruises' occurring very soon after children go out to play, may be because of the compelling need to run, climb and chase. Teachers who promoted greater use of the outdoors for longer periods during the day claimed that there were fewer accidents and improved behaviour. Recent research suggests that physical exercise improves the brain activity, moods and learning (Blakemore and Frith, 2005). This need does not suddenly disappear when the children move to Year One. I argue that teachers should consider the children's rights to access the outdoors for its own sake, and for the fulfilment of basic needs. It is possible to achieve this and to have a rich learning environment outdoors.

Discuss
- How can access to the outdoors be achieved with an appropriate level of risk?
- How can I convince parents and colleagues that the children should have 1) a right to experience the outdoors and 2) to take risks and develop skills to overcome obstacles?
- Do the children in Reception Class and Year One have enough time outdoors and a chance to play energetically?

The outdoors should not be considered as a less valuable learning environment than the indoors. One of the arguments used by schools to explain the lack of development in the outdoor environment is lack of funding. Thankfully, the rush to provide expensive soft surfaces to protect children has subsided. Even with acceptance that there must be safety and security outdoors, there also needs to be access to risk taking and natural resources. The outdoors is the largest part of the child's environment for life and they need to learn how to spend time in it. Before looking at examples of activities and resources that would enrich outdoor experiences, it is worth considering an argument for not spending too much money on it.

A basic plan for the outdoors that gives control to the children

If we invest money on road markings, pathways, pop-up tents and so on we are depriving children of opportunities to develop resourcefulness, creativity, collaboration and planning skills. We are also fixing the environment and limiting the variety of ways it can be used. To enable children to mark their own roads, paths and parking bays, using chalk, gives them opportunities for autonomy, creativity and to develop graphicacy skills. They have to measure and share space, calculate width for wheeled toys, design the layout and negotiate with their peers. Similarly if we provide ready-made shelters or tents, we deprive children of the pleasure and opportunities to develop skills in creating their own dens and shelters.

Figure 8.1 is a plan of a basic outdoor area in a primary school. In this example there are just a few simple structures that are permanent. The planters can be used to grow seasonal plants to develop children's knowledge and understanding of the cyclical nature of the seasons, in addition to the science of growing and nurturing. They might also be used to grow edible crops that could be incorporated into cooking activities. Winter and summer pansies are easy to grow and care for, providing colour all year. Runner beans provide colourful flowers and vegetables that can be harvested before school closes for the summer holiday. Strawberries can be grown in pots in confined spaces, provided they have sun. Different varieties will produce strawberries at different times of the year to suit requirements. Various herbs are easy to grow in pots and can be used for recipes, for instance mint, chives and dill.

The addition of a low raised area can transform the way children play. It can become a hill for 'I'm the king of the castle', a den of safe refuge during a game, a stage for a performance or other uses that creative children can develop. The table and shelf can also be used in a variety of ways for child-initiated activity or teacher-led learning. It can become the counter of a drive-through café, a garage/petrol station shop, the office for a campsite, the counter of a garden centre, the front for a puppet show and many other uses. Such a simple outdoor area can present a breadth of opportunities.

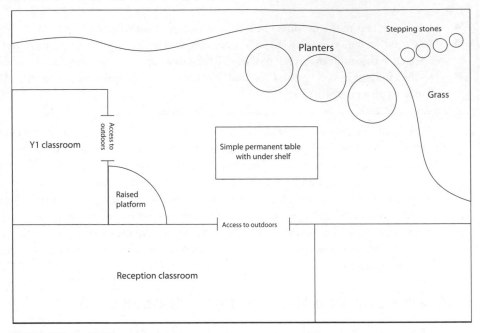

FIGURE 8.1 Basic outdoor area

Discuss
- What simple addition to the outdoors would improve the way children play outdoors?
- What resources can be added without cost?

Resourcing the outdoors

Resourcing the outdoors does not have to be complicated or expensive. Many resources that are used indoors, such as the apparatus for teaching mathematical concepts, can be used just as effectively outdoors. Mathematics can be done well outdoors. For instance, activities that involve the use of standard and non-standard measures, or estimating and measuring dimensions, can be done using the natural and built environment. Games or activities involving counting and the use of tally charts can be done outdoors with flip charts or whiteboards for recording. Shape can be explored within this environment using the features within it or using large resources, for instance to tessellate, for which there may not be adequate space indoors. For some children, the space to create 3D graphs using blocks will be more meaningful than the 2D version in an exercise book. Almost all aspects of the Key Stage One guidelines for mathematics can be addressed outdoors.

Discuss
- What mathematical activities could be carried out as effectively (or more effectively) outdoors rather than indoors?

Some teachers prefer to have some resources specifically identified for outdoor use that can be stored in wheeled trolleys or containers that can easily be transferred outdoors as required. For organisational purposes this is understandable. An example would be a container of resources for exploring and investigating, which could have clipboards, magnifying glasses, specimen pots and non-fiction books. The use of clipboards can engage some children in writing who may otherwise not have been inclined to do so: the added benefit of being outdoors makes it a little more engaging. For reluctant writers, writing for a purpose in which they will use their records to engage in a discussion about their findings has a positive impact. Cameras are a useful additional or alternative way to make records that can support recollection, reflection, discussion, retelling and writing. This is good for all children but especially appealing to those for whom the struggle to write *during* an activity can get in the way of them gaining insight. It can also demotivate them from an otherwise engaging activity. This applies to many children in Year One.

Discuss
- How can children take part fully and keep records of their activity without lengthy writing tasks?

There are many ways of promoting children's learning outdoors. However, below is a discussion of just two examples that can be used within Reception Class and developed to be more challenging for Year One to enable continuity and progression of provision.

Water and sand outdoors

Water and sand are important resources for Reception Class, often continuously available. They can be equally as important to children in Year One because they are familiar with the resource and are versatile. The use of water to develop children's understanding of its properties, floating and sinking, density, and to teach measures, is well known. Each of these can be further developed in Year One by extending the child's capacity to estimate, measure and articulate thoughts about scientific phenomena. There are other uses that can be suitably challenging for children in Year One, and which can be done effectively outdoors. The use of plastic pipes, gutters, buckets, tubes and water provide opportunities to discover more about the properties of water, for instance that it can be siphoned. These resources enable children to experiment with the movement of water, making links between capacity, velocity and gradient. The children can develop a hypothesis to test, and develop the vocabulary involved in enquiry. As with other activities children can record their work in different ways including collaborative writing on charts, note taking and photographs.

Wet sand, water and small world apparatus provide good resources for the development of graphicacy skills. Wet sand on large trays is an ideal resource for children to practice drawing plans and develop an understanding of the concept of scale. They can make roads in the sand and add cars from small world, or develop streets with houses. If they wish to add rivers or canals, water can be used to fill the channels they create. Clear-based trays enable them to place coloured paper beneath to represent road surfaces or water when the sand is displaced. An obvious advantage of using wet sand is that children can work together planning their small world, changing it as they develop their ideas. When they are ready they can attempt to draw on paper what they have created in sand, in the first steps to making maps. Further development of this could involve classroom plans and outdoor plans. Creating a treasure map including landmarks that other children can use to find hidden 'treasure' is an exciting way for children to develop their map-making skills.

Discuss
- Which learning objectives can be met through a treasure hunt?

Growing and nurturing plants outdoors

Children should experience growing their own plants from seeds, bulbs or cuttings and learn how to nurture them. Harvesting their own fruit and vegetables, and cooking and eating them are fulfilling things to do. As part of this theme there is a good opportunity to improve the understanding of non-fiction texts and style, and use of instructional texts. Teachers will be able to use this to challenge Year One children, including those who are making very good progress already. Below is a list of methods used by some teachers:

- studying the instructions on seed packets
- reading gardening books to select plants for their coloured flowers, foliage and season
- discussing the use of non-fiction texts to provide information about the care of plants, and the layout of the text;
- collaborative writing of instructions for the care of the garden area or planning tubs;
- using photographs to place in order for sequencing and retelling the story from sowing to harvesting;
- collaborative writing of a book telling the story;
- collaborative writing of instructions to tell others how to do the same;
- using recipes to use food grown and following the instructions;
- creating their own recipes using their own produce and recording these using photographs and writing instructions.

Discuss
- What do Year One teachers need to know about outdoor experiences the children have had in their previous year?
- How should this information be made available to them?
- How can the Year One teacher build on this, provide children with more access to the outdoors, and remain satisfied that the children will meet learning objectives expected for this phase?

Key messages

- The outdoors provides additional and alternative experiences for children to improve their knowledge and understanding of the world.
- Children are able to achieve learning objectives effectively in the outdoor environment.
- Children should have a right to access the outdoor environment.
- The outdoors provides space for energetic play, which is needed by young children.

Music

The reason I have chosen the subject of music as an issue during transition is because my own research found that there was limited provision for music in Reception Class and even less provision in Year One Classes. There are obvious exceptions to this, but it was found that where teachers lacked confidence in their own knowledge and skills in music the provision was more limited.

This section will look at why children should experience music before looking at the requirements of the national curriculum and how these can be addressed in an engaging way suited to the age and needs of the children.

Why children should experience music at school

When a wide range of teachers from Foundation Stage and Key Stage One were asked about their views on the provision of music in the classroom, they all stated that they thought it should definitely be included. However, although most of them stated that children enjoyed music, the other reasons offered were varied and indicated a lack of knowledge and conviction. One of them was that singing enabled children to join in and enjoy a sense of friendship. Music shared in group situations supports group identity (Pound, 2005). Children like to belong, and talking about what they sing together in school helps develop a sense of belonging. Music can express moods or create atmosphere. 'If you're happy and you know it clap your hands' is an obvious example of something children can join in, and it usually makes them smile. Similarly I have seen Rimsky Korsakov's 'Flight of the Bumble Bee' used to instil a sense of urgency and energy into tidy-up time. Calming music is sometimes used to change the mood of a class for reflection and meditation, and has the added benefit of bringing about desired behaviour.

The use of music to support learning in other subject areas was recognised by some teachers. Singing rhyming songs was seen as useful for developing phonological awareness, especially with silent cloze procedures when children are invited to supply a rhyming word. The use of songs with sequences and refrains was seen as very useful in supporting the understanding of rhythm, pattern and sequence. Endless counting songs are used and if percussion instruments were added they would add emphasis to the pattern and rhythm. Music also supports memory (Pound, 2005). A story set to music will aid the memory of the order of events. Children will associate particular pieces of music with particular memories, so that it is helpful for recall. In addition to the sense of belonging already mentioned, music can be a useful resource for the development of social skills in children. For instance, traditional nursery rhymes to music and movement can encourage turn taking. An example of this is 'In and Out the Dusty Bluebells' in which children take turns to go 'in and out' then choose someone to have a turn by tapping them on the shoulder. I have an aversion to 'looking through rose-tinted glasses' as I believe children's experiences should relate to the world *they* were born into, not that of the adults in charge. However, lessons can be learned from the past, and the ballroom style dance routines and other sequence dances experienced in the primary classroom many years ago served well to develop an understanding of cooperation, turn taking, and social protocol. It might be argued that it supported the brain's developing capacity for memory.

Learning about music for its own sake was seldom given as a reason for its provision in the case study settings. Children need to learn about different sounds, pitch and volume, and be able to compose simple pieces. Understanding the dynamics of music and the creativity involved is important for the children. They need to understand how sounds can be created using different materials and objects. They need to be able to explore how the properties of materials link to the sounds, for instance the difference between hollow metal and soft fabrics. The various purposes of music can be explored through drama, for example music for dance and for lullabies. There is a danger that the natural gift of musical ability in some children may go unnoticed if there are insufficient opportunities to explore it.

Discuss

- What reasons are there for improving the provision of music in both Reception Class and Year One?
- How can this be progressive between the two phases?
- How could I incorporate more music into the classroom?
- How can children be encouraged to listen to and discuss music?
- Are children able to select and play music of their choice?

Fulfilling the requirement to provide musical experiences

The attainment targets set out by the national curriculum for maintained schools, in Key Stage One are shown below.

LEVEL 1

Pupils recognise and explore how sounds can be made and changed. They use their voices in different ways such as speaking, singing and chanting, and perform with awareness of others. They repeat short rhythmic and melodic patterns and create and choose sounds in response to given starting points. They respond to different moods in music and recognise well-defined changes in sounds, identify simple repeated patterns and take account of musical instructions.

LEVEL 2

Pupils recognise and explore how sounds can be organised. They sing with a sense of the shape of the melody, and perform simple patterns and accompaniments keeping to a steady pulse. They choose carefully and order sounds within simple structures such as beginning, middle, end, and in response to given starting points. They represent sounds with symbols and recognise how the musical elements can be used to create different moods and effects. They improve their own work.

The following is a list of activities that have been observed in Key Stage One that would address curriculum requirements and, most importantly, engage and support the children's learning and skill development effectively. It is assumed that prior to these the children will have had ample opportunity in Reception Class to join in singing, use simple instruments to mark a rhythm, participate in songs with refrains and talk about music that makes them feel happy or sad. The notes are intentionally brief as they are ideas for teachers and not plans.

1. STAIRS

A simple tune such as the 'Do-re-mi' song from *The Sound of Music*, or any song or tune in which there is an obvious movement up or down a scale can be used for this simple activity. When the music rises up the full scale during 'Do-re-mi-fa-so-la-ti-do' the children gradually move up in the manner of climbing a stair for each note. The same happens in reverse for the descending scale.

2. VOLUME BUTTON

Firstly listen to recorded music and discuss the changes in volume introducing the vocabulary, for instance loud and quiet, and putting the volume up or down. Children often confuse pitch and volume when adults talk about going up or down. We often say 'turn that music down' when we mean 'turn the volume down'. Once they have grasped the link between volume 'up' and 'louder', and 'down' and 'quieter' they will be ready to explore volume. A simple game that will engage them is to have a group of children to sing a very simple familiar song, for instance 'The Grand Old Duke of York', perhaps repeating it. Children can have a turn at being the conductor, indicating an increase in volume by widening the arms, and decreasing volume by returning the arms close to the body.

3. MOVEMENT IN RESPONSE TO CHANGING PITCH

Use classical music, for example Vaughan William's 'The Lark Ascending', to which children move freely in response to what they hear. This piece of music has changes in pitch representing the movement of the bird in the sky, which would not be difficult for children to recognise.

4. RESPONDING TO CHANGES IN TEMPO.

Through teacher direction and free movement children can respond to changes in tempo.

5. THE USE OF MUSIC IN STORYTELLING.

'In the Hall of the Mountain King' from Grieg's *Peer Gynt* has been used frequently, perhaps because the music is dramatic and conjures a picture from the story. The slow, careful steps Peer Gynt takes are represented by cellos and bassoons; the entrance of the king's trolls is represented by an upwards change in pitch. The tempo speeds up and volume increases as the trolls chase Peer Gynt. Long notes on strings represent the king's slow footsteps as he looks for Peer Gynt. Increasingly loud and fast music indicates the frantic escape from the cave, followed by clashing cymbals and loud drums as the cave collapses behind him. The slightly melancholy music at the end represents Peer's return to safety. Teachers would have to judge the children's ability to cope with the story. Using a small selection of samples from Saint-Saëns' *Carnival of the Animals* to discuss with the children how different instruments and sounds have been used to represent various animals may be useful. The 'March of the Lion' is bold and stately music that could be associated with a 'king' status. The slow music of the tortoise is evident in its relevance, as is the use of a double bass for the elephant.

Children create a story, using sounds from within the environment, instruments available to them and/or recorded music. To present a challenge to those who are able, there are opportunities to plan and write stories, create sounds or select music to accompany a short story, and use ICT to record the process and end product. The purpose of recording would be for evaluation during and after the process and for performance.

6. DISCUSSION ABOUT MUSIC

It is important for teachers to enable children to share thoughts and ideas about music. This may include discussions about preferences, the impact on feelings, appreciation and evaluation of their own and others' work.

7. CHILDREN LIKE TO PERFORM

Through play children can plan, rehearse and perform. In addition to developing their skills in music and movement, it provides opportunities for the development of leadership and organisational skills, and confidence in front of an audience. A more formal performance in which there is teacher involvement is also appropriate.

8. ACCOMPANY RECORDED MUSIC WITH NON-TUNED PERCUSSION

The use of recorded music with regular rhythms, and with simple and obvious changes to rhythm, for children to accompany with percussion is a simple thing to organise.

Discuss
- Could I improve the opportunities for children to learn about music?
- Could I make greater use of music for other purposes such as emotional expression?
- Should the children have a right to listen to and create their own music?
- How could this be achieved?
- Could I use music to encourage collaborative behaviour?

Key messages

- Teachers do not need to have expertise in music in order to provide interesting and challenging musical experiences for children.
- Music has a strong impact on how children feel.
- Music can enable children to express themselves and be creative.
- Music is a useful medium through which other subjects can be taught.

Time management

Issues with time management for Reception teachers and teachers of Year One are often about providing enough time for children to play. The anxiety is often about needing enough time for themselves to work with the children so that they can be certain that the children address learning objectives, and a corresponding lack of confidence in the role of free play in meeting those objectives. Confidence in the role of play will be addressed in the next section. This section will look at why teachers need to rethink the organisation of the day and what barriers there are to achieving this.

In the case study schools included in previous chapters, the only complaint that children expressed verbally was about abrupt interruptions to their play. The other aspect over which they showed similar signs of discontent was the length of time they spent on adult-directed activity. In Reception Class it was the interruption to play that was the main issue and in Year One it was the discontent with the length of time on adult-directed activities that was more evident. Ironically, it was the teachers' efforts to enable children to have free play that contributed to the abrupt interruptions to that play. The Reception teachers tended to have free access to play for much of the day, but called children individually or in small groups to sit with them while they did focused adult-led sessions. Those called at the start of the morning or afternoons were unaffected. Sadly others, who had become deeply engaged in their play, exhibited frustration when called away from it. In the Year One Classes there was more likely to be clearly defined times of work and free play, so that although time for play was limited, it was at least uninterrupted. In Year One, there was a greater tendency to have longer periods of time in which children had to sit and listen to the teacher; this was uncomfortable and unproductive for many children.

Barriers to achieving a balance of good quality adult-led, child-initiated and child-and-adult activities, perceived by the teachers, are about external pressures. Teachers are affected by a need to comply with the school timetabled events such as playtime, lunchtime, school assembly and use of indoor space, for instance the hall. They are concerned about meeting targets and often organise the day in an attempt to ensure they work with children to achieve these. These factors dominate the time management of the teachers, rather than pedagogy.

Discuss
- How can Year One teachers improve the adult-led sessions so that they are interactive and of shorter duration?
- Is it possible to plan the timetable to have uninterrupted periods of play and still have quality adult inputs?
- Would it be better to have fewer opportunities to play but longer duration?
- What impact might changes have on other classes in Key Stage One (e.g. breaks)?

Key messages
- It is not just the amount of time given to various aspects of provision that matters, but the duration of those time slots.

Play

Throughout this book there have been several references to play, its benefits to children and some difficulties encountered in providing it. Regarding transition issues, the first chapter stated that the biggest challenge identified by teachers was the move from a play-based curriculum to a more structured approach. My own research found that although teachers said that they knew play was important and believed children should be allowed to play, they lacked confidence in two aspects:

1. whether the children would meet the required learning objectives through play and
2. how they should be involved in and support learning through play.

Therefore, this concluding section returns to the subject of play. In order to attempt to address the above, it will look at how play supports learning in the three curriculum areas in which, traditionally, successful achievement is measured. This measured achievement of the children impacts on teachers who feel accountable. Therefore, the teachers may feel inclined to use formal methods in which they are in control and can be certain that learning objectives are being met. This section will look at how play also supports learning in literacy and language, mathematics and science. It will not validate the use of play in terms of its suitability for children, as this has been addressed elsewhere. It will focus on practical suggestions observed through case studies referred to in earlier chapters.

Literacy and language through play

Literacy and language can be developed effectively through play because it is easier for children to engage in language if it is meaningful and in context. Play is especially important for the development of speaking and listening skills. For obvious reasons it is better to introduce new vocabulary in context. For instance, if children have stethoscopes to use in role play, they will have no difficulty in recalling the name of the instrument. Children, like adults, need to 'talk things through', to articulate their thoughts in order to clarify a concept. By interacting with other children (and sometimes adults) during play they will share ideas, learn to see other's perspectives and develop thought. Many children will find this easier to do during informal activity than in a formal group task. It could also be argued that play provides children with an opportunity to take time out to think, rather than in a formal situation when the teacher may expect a more immediate response to a suggestion or question.

Play is a useful way for children to learn about the use of spoken and written language when conveying information and meaning to others. With subtle support, they can learn that there are different ways to express the spoken and written language depending on the purpose. 'Walkie-talkie' toys and telephones can introduce conventions used in audio communication. A notepad left by the telephone in the role play area could encourage note taking during 'telephone conversations', for instance if it were a doctor's surgery. Taking orders in a café or writing a shopping list for a picnic or party give purpose and techniques for writing, and introduce the conventions for speech between shopkeeper and customer. Learning about different ways to greet or send greetings can be learned through play. I suggest the adults' role would be one of participation and example in such circumstances, rather than instruction. Imitation is a crucial part of learning. Through imitation children not only learn the basic knowledge and skills, but how these sit in context. It is the context that provides meaning and an opportunity to make connections with previous experiences and knowledge.

The environment can be enriched to encourage children to engage in speaking and listening, writing and reading. The addition of fiction and non-fiction books and writing equipment to various areas of the classroom environment (indoors and outdoors) will help prevent the separation of such activities from play. Some of these may have been introduced during adult-led sessions and are available for the children to use for consolidation during play. Books created by the children can be part of the play, rather than being displayed and unused. For instance, a book of recipes, mentioned in Chapter 7, could be included in a home corner or café. Message boards with dry marker pens would encourage children to write messages, price lists, opening times, duty rosters etc., some of which will come from outside school and can be shared.

ICT within play areas will also support the development of literacy and language skills. Apart from the use of commercial software for this purpose, there are other simple uses that enhance this subject area. For instance the use of digital photography for the development of stories, digital picture frames for images to stimulate conversation and thought, and recording devices to encourage spoken language and listening skills are effective. The use of technology to record speech provides an opportunity for the child to evaluate his/her own work and consider improvements.

Discuss
- Are there any planned lessons for literacy and language that could be achieved through play?
- Would you have confidence in achieving the learning objectives?
- What would the teacher's role be?
- What professional development (if any) would teachers and/or support staff need to improve the use of play for learning in this subject?
- How would you assess and evaluate learning through play?

Mathematics through play

Mathematics should be introduced carefully to children. The case study of Chris in Chapter 2 was about a child who enjoyed mathematical activities in Reception Class. He enjoyed mathematical games and liked to articulate his thoughts about number games, and about measures in the sand and water area. However, the formal approach of his Year One Class meant that all mathematical concepts were introduced during teacher-led whole class or large group sessions. During such sessions the children were given techniques to answer sums, so that many of them such as Chris could complete a set of sums quickly, as they recognised a pattern. If the pattern or the way it was illustrated changed, Chris was unable to complete the task and lost confidence. Processes are just as important as facts in mathematics (Sarama and Clements, 2009). Children need to experience the processes that lead to the recording of sums if they are to make sense. Sarama and Clements (2009) argue that 'curiosity, imagination, inventiveness, risk-taking, creativity, and persistence – are components of the essential productive disposition' (p4). If we cut straight to the facts and miss out the important processes, children will not understand the concepts and will not develop positive dispositions to engage happily and successfully in mathematical activities. Through play and sensitive adult support children can continue to use curiosity, imagination, risk taking and so on (that they should have developed in Reception Class) to improve their developing understanding of mathematical concepts.

There are far too many ideas for practical activities and play to go into detail in this chapter. However, it is worthwhile looking at some simple ways of resourcing and supporting play in Year One that will provide continuity from Reception Class and will also be adequately challenging. Each of these would require further consideration and are simply starting points:

- *Construction blocks* provide an ideal resource for estimating and measuring length and breadth. They can support developing understanding of symmetry, circumference, radii and 3D shapes. Adult involvement can introduce the vocabulary of names and properties of each of these.

- *Sand and water* will be familiar to the children and their already established understanding of capacity can be further developed through use of standard and non-standard measures, estimates and comparisons. The latter provides opportunities for calculations through meaningful activities. Nearby writing resources allow recording of simple calculations made by comparison.

- *A set of scales* in the home corner, shop or baby clinic can be used for real measures. There is no reason why a child should not begin to understand real measures. For instance a 2kg bag of potatoes or 1kg bag of sugar gives a good idea what such a weight feels like. Reading labels on packages to find the weight will give a true understanding of weight and measure. A child is more likely to recall measures used for a baking exercise than in reading a book about it.

- *Time* is a concept that needs to be taught through normal processes. The use of real clocks in the environment to measure how much time children can have in a given area, or how long there is until lunchtime will soon give the children a sound understanding of what, for instance, half an hour feels like. Opening times for the shop, appointment times at the clinic or the length of time something must be left in the oven provide meaningful experiences and support learning.

- *A haberdashery, tailor or dressmaker role play* can provide for several mathematical concepts. Buttons can be sorted according to size, shape or colour and counted. Ribbon could be available in different colours, widths and patterns. Lengths of fabric can be used to measure length and width, to estimate lengths required for a purpose and as appropriate to discuss repeating patterns. The inclusion of a height chart would be similar to those used in children's clothes shops where clothing is sometimes sold by height. Children can examine clothes labels to pursue this. The use of real measuring tapes adds authenticity.

- *Money* can be used in role play areas such as shops and cafés. Real coins could be used to 'purchase' drinks and snacks. Adult support can be used to differentiate this as needed.

FIGURE 8.2 A budding scientist

- *Shape* may be explored in a variety of ways through play, arguably more effectively than using manufactured shapes for formal teaching. Different shapes of containers, cake tins, plates, stencils for decorating cakes or for craft activities, pastry cutters and the natural environment provide endless stimuli for discussion about the properties of 2D and 3D shapes.

Discuss
- How would you support a developing understanding of spending money and obtaining change from 10p and 20p?
- How might this be recorded in a way that the child will understand?
- Are there any aspects of mathematics that cannot be learned through play?
- How would a teacher monitor children's grasp of new mathematical concepts?
- How would you plan a role play area in Year One that would support mathematical development? How would you ensure that the children are challenged?

Science through play

Science needs a safe risk-taking environment that allows budding scientists to develop a scientific brain by exploring, investigating and inventing. Transition from Reception Class to Year One should be a smooth one from scientific exploration to enquiry (Howe and Davies, 2005).

Such enquiry might follow a pattern as follows:

Observe or notice ⇨ explore ⇨ discuss and record ⇨ predict (ask what if?) ⇨ try or experiment ⇨ observe and reflect on what has been learned ⇨ what next? new questions?

An example of how children can be supported in developing an enquiry is that of forces and the velocity of small world wheeled vehicles. This can begin with children observing the movement of cars and talking about how fast they are going, and making comparisons. The teacher would model recording which car is the fastest on a whiteboard or clipboard.

The children would then be encouraged to predict what would happen if the surface was altered and try this, observe, discuss and record. A discussion would follow about what was observed and why this may have happened. It might involve the properties of the new surface. The children would then be encouraged to propose new questions to explore and investigate, which could include the effect of gradient, or adding weight to a car and so on.

The process of noticing and observing, asking questions, predicting, trying or testing, discussing what has been observed, suggesting reasons, and forming new questions can be applied to many situations, planned and spontaneous. The following examples are simple ideas that could be developed to challenge Year One children so that they will improve scientific knowledge and develop scientific skills of enquiry:

- *Life-processes* can be explored using magnifying glasses to look closely at germinating seeds, opening buds, and the different vein patterns on leaves, moving insects, a spider's web and many other purposes. Planting, nurturing and, when relevant, harvesting plants helps develop knowledge and understanding of life processes.
- *The elements* can be explored and investigated by blowing bubbles and observing their movement, kite flying, finding out about evaporation by hanging out 'washing' to see whether the sun or wind is most effective in drying it, making parachutes with different materials and investigating the properties of snow.
- *Water* can be investigated for buoyancy, movement and changing properties when heated or cooled, or when ingredients are added.
- *Safe access to real machinery* for children to investigate, dismantle, reinvent or replicate enables children to investigate cogs, wheels and springs and their relationship with force and movement.
- *Construction area* is an ideal place to explore pulleys and levers, and try new materials and resources to construct levers and pulleys for a purpose. This can be investigated on a large scale outdoors.

Discuss
- How can I turn the children into 'budding scientists'?
- Is it possible to develop a scientific culture in the classroom where children feel free to explore, investigate, invent and make mistakes?

Key messages
- Literacy and language, mathematics and science can be taught effectively through play.
- Many aspects of these subjects are taught more effectively through play if well planned and supported.

CHAPTER

9

Summary and recommendations

There are definitely issues to address around the subject of transition from Reception Class to Year One. It is vital to get the right approach, as the fostering of positive dispositions to learning will have a long-term impact on each child. This book has examined some of the issues. However, greater emphasis has been placed on a more positive approach, that is, to view the transition period as chance to reflect and change. The children from the case study examples each had varying experiences of the transition process, and this was partly because of their different needs; this will always be a considerable factor. The other most evident factor was the impact of knowledge and external pressures on the philosophy and practice of the teachers. The number of years experience did not always correlate with confidence or effectiveness. However, those who were better informed about research into how young children learn had stronger convictions and more confidence in their practice. Even for these teachers, there was an overriding factor that could exert a greater influence on their practice: the external pressure of colleagues and line managers.

In order for transition between the two phases of education to be an opportunity to improve experiences for young children, it is vital that those involved should at least engage in critical reflection. Suggestions as to how this might be achieved have been made in this book. Sharing thoughts with others improves our own reflections and transforms knowledge. Arguably the most useful form of professional development is action research, which 'is concerned with improvement and change, with achieving now what otherwise might remain unrealised' (Schratz and Walker, 1995: 75). Discussions about action research usually include the notions of collaboration, participation, empowerment, social change and acquisition of knowledge (Cook, 2009). A network of communities, in which Reception Class and Year One teachers from neighbouring schools meet, would provide opportunities to share experiences and undertake enquiry.

'Cognitively, information becomes knowledge through people working together in solving problems and achieving goals, and knowledge becomes shared wisdom through sustained interaction' (Li, 2008: 251). Involvement of line managers in this learning community would achieve a consensus of opinion on a) what effective practice should look like, b) a shared philosophy, c) improved confidence and d) improved conviction. When teachers gain more knowledge they become empowered and more able to challenge resistance to change. In simple terms they are no longer just able to say what should be done, but will be confident in the knowledge of 'why'. It is the latter that is essential if teachers are to be committed to bringing about improvements.

Collaborative research is often linked to teaching practice. According to Savoie–Zajc and Descamps–Bernarz (2007) there are two perspectives. The first of these is a spirit of reflexive community that impacts on practice and the atmosphere of the school. The second is the recognition of the gap between the professional practice and the research that is intended to inform it. When teachers' practice is informed by research from the academic world and their own collaborative enquiry this gap closes. When reflecting with other educational professionals, new viewpoints are introduced, and in turn lead to further reflection. This helps teachers to see things from different perspectives, and supports the development of new knowledge, with the knowledge and experience we already have. The most important message is that teachers should work together to take a critically reflective approach to transition, viewing it as an opportunity to reflect and make improvements.

References

Adams, S., Alexander, E., Drummond, M.J. and Myles, J. (2004) *Inside the Foundation Stage, Recreating the Reception Year*, London: ATL Publications.

Anderson, H. with Adlam, T., Coltman, P., Daniels, R. and Linklater, H. (2003) 'Spinning the Plates', in Whitebread, D. (ed.) *Teaching and Learning in the Early Years*, London: Routledge Falmer

Barnard, J. (2006) 'The Nesting Instinct', *The Guardian*, April.

Blakemore, S. J. and Frith, U. (2005) *The Learning Brain: Lessons for Education*, Oxford: Blackwell Publishing.

Bolton, G. (2010) *Reflective Practice. Writing and Professional Development*, London: Sage Publications.

Broadhead, P. (2007) 'Working Together to Support Playful Learning and Transition', in Moyles, J. (ed.) *Early Years Foundations: Meeting the Challenge*, Maidenhead: Open University Press.

Broadhead, P. and English, C. (2005) 'Open-ended Role Play: Supporting Creativity and Developing Identity', in Moyles, J. (ed.) *The Excellence of Play, 2nd edition*, Maidenhead: Open University Press.

Bronfenbrenner, U. (1995) 'Developmental Ecology Through Space and Time: A Future Perspective', in Moen, P et al. (eds) *Examining Lives in Context: Perspectives on the Ecology of Human Development*, Washington DC: American Psychological Association, 619–647.

Brooker, L. (2001) 'Interviewing Children', in MacNaughton, G., Rolfe, S. and Siraj-Blatchford, I. (eds) *Doing Early Childhood Research: International Perspectives on Theory and Practice*, Buckingham: Open University Press.

Bruner, J. (1980) *Under Five in Britain*, London: Grant MacIntyre Publishers.

Buchbinder, M., Longhofer, J., Barrett, T., Lawson, P. and Floersch, J. (2006) 'Ethnographic Approaches to Child Care Research', *Journal of Early Childhood Research* 2006, 4(1), 45–63.

CACE (Central Advisory Council for Education) (1967) *Children and their Primary Schools (The Plowden Report)*, London: HMSO.

Campbell, S. (2005) 'Secret Children's Business. Resisting and Redefining Access to Learning in the Early Childhood Classroom', in Yelland, N. (ed.) *Critical Issues in Early Childhood Education*, Maidenhead: Open University Press.

Carr, M. (2002) 'Emerging Learning Narratives: A Perspective from Early Childhood Education', in Wells, G. and Claxton, G. (eds) *Learning for Life in the 21st Century*, Oxford: Blackwell Publishers.

Carruthers, E. (2007) 'Children's Outdoor Experiences: A Sense of Adventure', in Moyles, J. (ed.) *Early Years Foundations Meeting the Challenge*, Maidenhead: Open University Press.

Claxton, G. (1999) *Wise Up: The Challenge of Lifelong Learning*, Stafford: Network Learning Press Ltd.

Claxton, G. (2002) *Building Learning Power*, Bristol: TLO Publications.

Cook, T. (2009) 'The purpose of mess in action research: building rigours through messy turn.' *Educational Action Research* 17.2.277-291. London: Routledge.

David, T. (2003) *What do we know about teaching young children?*, Professional User Review Series, Southwell: British Educational Research Association.

DCSF (2008) *Early Years Inundation Stage*, London: QCA Publications.

Dennett, D.C. (1995) *Darwin's Dangerous Idea: Evolution and the Meanings of Life*, London: Allen Lane, The Penguin Press.

Dewey, J. (1938) *Experience and Education*, 1997 edition, Touchstone: New York.

DfCSF (2008) *Primary National Strategies: Talk for Writing*. Nottingham: DCSF Publications.

DfEE (1999) *All our Futures; Creativity, Culture and Education*. National Advisory Committee on Creative and Cultural Education. NACCCE Report.

DfEE (2000) *Curriculum Guidance for the Foundation Stage*, London: QCA Publications.

DfES (2003) *Foundation Stage Profile Handbook*, Sudbury: QCA Publications.

DfES (2005) *Social and Emotional Aspects of Learning (SEAL): Improving Behaviour, Improving Learning*, London: QCA Publications.

DfES (2006) *Seamless Transitions – Supporting Continuity in Young Children's Learning*, London: DfES publications.

Dockett, S., Perry, B., Howard, P. and Meckley, A. (1999) 'What do early childhood educators and parents think is important about children's transition to school? A comparison between data from the city and the bush,' paper presented at the Australian Association for Research in Education Annual Conference, Melbourne, 29 November – 2 December, http://www.aare.edu.au/99pap/per99541.htm (accessed 26th August, 2006).

Edmund, R. (2005) 'Ethnographic research methods with children and young people', in Greene, S. and Hogan, D. (eds) *Researching Children's Experiences*, London: Sage Publications.

Ellis, S. (2005) 'Mind your language', *Nursery World*, 24 February, 12–13.

English, E. (2001) 'Teaching for understanding: curriculum for the foundation stage', *Evaluation and Research in Education* 15(3), 197–204.

Eriksson, E.H. (1950) *Childhood and Society*, New York: Norton.

Eyles, J. (2007) 'Vision, mission method, challenges and issues in developing the role of the early years mentor teacher', in Moyles, J. (ed.) *Early Years Foundations: Meeting the Challenge*, Maidenhead: Open University Press.

Fabian, H. (2005) 'Outdoors learning environments: Easing the transition from the Foundation Stage to Key Stage One', *Education* 3–13 33(2), 4–8.

Fisher, J.A. (2009) 'We used to play in Foundation – It was more funner: Investigating feelings about transition from Foundation Stage to Year 1, *Early Years* 29(2), 131–145.

Fisher, R. (1995) *Teaching Children to Learn*, Cheltenham: Stanley Thornes Publishers.

Harding, S. (2005) 'Outdoor play and the pedagogic garden', in Moyles, J. (ed.) *The Excellence of Play*, 2nd edition, Maidenhead: Open University Press.

Haywood, H.C. (2004) 'Thinking in, around and about the curriculum: The role of cognitive education', *International Journal of Disability, Development, and Education* 51(3), 231–252.

Henry, M. (2004) 'Developmental needs and early childhood education: Evolutionary, my ear Watson', *Early Child Development and Care* 174(4), 301–312.

Howe, A. and Davies, D. (2005) 'Science and play', in Moyles, J. (ed.) *The Excellence of Play*, 2nd edition, Maidenhead: Open University Press.

IFF Research (2004) *Transition from Foundation Stage to Key Stage One*, research prepared for DfES/Sure Start, February, London: IFF Research Ltd.

Jarvis, P. (2007) 'Monsters, magic and Mr Psycho: A Biocultural approach to rough and tumble play in the early years of primary school', *Early Years* 27(2), 171–188.

Katz, L. (2004) 'Bridging the gap', presented at the Institute of Education conference, University of London, October.

Kendall, L., Morrison, J., Sharp, C. and Yeshanew, T. (2008) *The Impact of Creative Partnerships on Pupil Behaviour*, NFER.

Kylin, M. (2003) 'Children's dens', *Children, Youth and Environments* 13(1), 1–25.

Li, Y.-L. (2008) 'Teachers in action research: Assumptions and potentials', *Educational Action Research* 16(2), 251–260.

Lofdahl, A. (2006) 'Grounds for values and attitudes, children's play and peer-cultures in pre-school', *Journal of Early Childhood Research* 4(1), 77–88.

Lopez, F., Menez, M. and Hernandez-Guzman, L. (2005) 'Sustained attention during learning activities: An observational study with pre-school children', *Early Child Development and Care* 175(2), 131–138.

MacNaughton, G., Smith, K. and Lawrence, H. (2003) *Children's Strategy – Consulting with Children Birth to Eight Years of Age. Hearing Young Children's Voices*, London: Children's Services Branch, ACT Department of Education, Youth and Family Services.

May, P., Ashford, E. and Bottle, G. (2006) *Sound Beginnings: Learning and Development in the Early Years*, London: David Fulton Publishers.

Maynard, T. and Waters, J. (2007) 'Learning in the outdoor environment: A missed opportunity?' *Early Years* 27(3) 255–265.

Mezirow, J. and associates (1990) *Fostering Critical Reflection in Adulthood*, San Francisco, CA: Jossey-Bass.

Moon, J. (1999) *Reflection in Learning and Professional Development: Theory and Practice*, Oxon: RoutledgeFalmer.

Moyles, J. (ed.) (2005) *The Excellence of Play*, 2nd edition, Maidenhead: Open University Press.

Moyles, J., Adams, S. and Musgrove, A. (2002) *Study of Pedagogical Effectiveness in Early Learning (SPEEL)*, Research Report RR 363, London: DfES Publications.

Nurse, A. (2001) 'A question of inclusion', in Abbott, L. and Nutbrown, C. (eds) *Experiencing Reggio Emilia: Implications for Pre-school Provision*, Maidenhead: Open University Press.

Nutbrown, C. (1994) *Threads of Thinking, 2nd edition*, London: Paul Chapman Publishing.

Ofsted (2004) *Transition for the Reception Year to Year 1: An evaluation by HMI*. HMI 2221.

Ofsted (2006) *Creative Partnerships: Initiatives and Impact*, HMI 2517.

Ouvry, M. (2003) *Exercising Muscles and Minds: Outdoor Play and the Early Years Curriculum*, London: National Early Years Network.

Piaget, J. (1998) *Jean Piaget: Selected Works*, 3rd edition, London: Routledge.

Pollard, A. (2002) *Reflective Teaching: Effective and Evidence-informed Professional Practice*, London: Continuum.

Pound, L. (2005) 'Playing music', in Moyles, J. (ed.) *The Excellence of Play*, 2nd edition, Maidenhead: Open University Press.

Radford, M. (1999) 'Co-constructing reality: The child's understanding of the world', in David, T. (ed.) *Young Children Learning,* London: Paul Chapman Publishing.

Robbins, J. (2005) 'Interweaving the Stitch and the Fabric: A Sociocultural Perspective on Researching Children's Thinking', paper presented at the British Educational Research Association Conference, Pontypridd, Wales, September.

Ryan, S. (2005) 'Freedom to choose: Examining children's experiences in choice time', in Yelland, N. (ed.) *Critical Issues in Early Childhood Education*, Maidenhead: Open University Press.

Safford, K. and O'Sullivan, O. (2007). *Their Learning Becomes Your Journey: Parents Respond to Children's Work in Creative Partnerships*, UK: Centre for Literacy in Primary Education.

Sanders, D., White, G., Burge, B., Sharp, C., Eames, A., McEnne, R. and Grayson, H. (2005) *A Study of the Transition from the Foundation Stage to Key Stage One,* DfES Research Report SSU/2005/FR/013, London: QCA Publications.

Sarama, J. and Clements, D.H. (2009) *Early Childhood Mathematics, Education Research, Learning Trajectories for Young Children*, Routledge: Abingdon.

Savoie-Zajc, L. and Descamps-Bednarz, N. (2007) 'Action research and collaborative research: Their specific contributions to professional development', *Educational Action Research* 15(4), 577–596.

Schratz, M. and Walker, R. (1995) *Research as Social Change: New Opportunities for Qualitative Research*, Oxon: Routledge.

Shier, H. (2001) 'Pathways to participation: Openings, opportunities and obligations', *Children & Society* 15, 107–117.

Shin, M.S., Recchia, S.L., Lee, S.Y., Lee Y.J. and Mullarkey, L.S. (2004) 'Understanding early childhood leadership', *Journal of Early Childhood Research* 2(3), 301–316.

Siraj-Blatchford, I., Sylva, K., Taggart, B., Sammons, P., Melhuish, E. and Elliot, K. (2003) 'Intensive Case Studies of Practice across the Foundation Stage', *The Effective Provision of Pre-school Education Project (EPPE),* Technical paper 10, University of London: Institute of Education.

Smith, P.K. (2005) 'Physical activity and rough-and-tumble play', in Moyles, J. (ed.) *The Excellence of Play*, 2nd edition, Maidenhead: Open University Press.

United Nations (1989) Convention on the Rights of the Child.

Vygotsky, L. (1992) *Thought and Language*, revised edition, Cambridge, MA: MIT Press.

Waters, J. and Begley, S. (2007) 'Supporting the development of risk-taking behaviours in the early years: An exploratory study', *Education 3–13* 35(3), 365–377.

Westcott, H.L. and Littleton, K.S. (2005) 'Exploring Meaning in Interviews with Children', in Greene, S. and Hogan, D. (eds) *Researching Children's Experience: Approaches and Methods*, London: Sage Publications.

White, G. and Sharp, C. (2007) '"It is different…because you are getting older and growing up." How children make sense of the transition to Year 1', *European Early Childhood Research* 15(1), 87–102.

Index